NATIONAL PARKS OF SWEDEN

Dear Dentiua

with my sincere thanks for your dedicated
contributions to make ECDC's work more
pertinent for the countries. We will sorely
miss your wisdom and energy!

In case you'd like to see more of Sweden
than Stockholm this book might be a
good excuse to come back.

All the best

Andrea

Mike

© Bokförlaget Max Ström
www.maxstrom.se
Text: Claes Grundsten
© The photos: Claes Grundsten, except pp. 78–79 (Martin Almqvist)
www.fotograf-grundsten.se
Front cover: Vadvetjåkka national park
Back cover: Djurö national park
Page 6: Pasque flowers in Stenshuvud national park
Translation: Greg McIvor
Design: Patric Leo
Layout: Patric Leo, Petra Ahston Inkapööl
Map: Martin Thelander
Printing: Elanders Fälth & Hässler, Hungary 2014
Second impression
ISBN 978-91-7126-156-4

NATIONAL PARKS OF SWEDEN

Claes Grundsten

Bokförlaget Max Ström

CONTENTS

On May 24, 2009, it was exactly one hundred years since the inauguration of Sweden's first national parks. They were the first national parks in Europe and marked the beginning of the continent's conservation movement. Today there are twenty-nine Swedish national parks and taken together they present a magnificent spectrum of the very best the Swedish countryside has to offer.

The purpose of the national parks is to protect valuable habitats and species, as well as to enrich the way people appreciate and commune with nature – both now and in the future. They also provide unique opportunities for environmental research. Many of our national parks have "climate archives" that are key to our understanding of how climatic changes affect man and our environment. The Royal Swedish Academy of Sciences has a research station at Abisko National Park that offers outstanding scope for studying climate impacts through changes in vegetation. Likewise, the glaciers of Sarek National Park are a significant historical databank, while the bogs of other national parks also provide important clues for climate researchers.

This book is a magnificent journey through the many natural environments that the national parks represent. The journey is a reminder of the importance of caring for our countryside and wildlife and managing it prudently. My hope is that this will inspire increased awareness in the wonder of our natural environments and strengthen our will to take responsibility for Planet Earth, our shared home.

His Majesty King Carl XVI Gustaf

WHY NATIONAL PARKS?

Sweden's national parks celebrate their centenary in 2009. The initial group of nine parks, founded back in 1909, were the first of their kind in Europe and marked out Sweden as a trailblazer in the continent's nascent conservation movement. With large areas of untouched countryside and spectacular scenery, Sweden was well suited to become the cradle of European conservation. Vast forests and rugged mountains made ideal national parks, especially as much of the land was state-owned. Swedes also take an instinctive interest in the nature and culture around them – and this served as a fertile basis for conservation ideals. The Swedish Tourist Association, founded in 1885, actively promoted public awareness of nature and cultural heritage. Local preservation societies were also strong during this era, and respected writers waxed lyrical about the delights of the Swedish countryside. Crucially, a group of leading scientists based mainly in Uppsala was able to exploit strong political connections to win backing for successful conservation initiatives. The same year that the first national parks opened also saw the birth of the Swedish Society for the Conservation of Nature.

This was also an age of nationalism, and the new cluster of national parks was a demonstration of love and pride in the motherland. The original idea came from the United States, where Yellowstone became the world's first national park in 1872. Yet the philosophy of protecting special natural habitats was not new even then. For thousands of years, man's relationship with nature has been connected to religious beliefs, and sacred sites have often been accorded special protection. Trees growing beside Chinese temples have traditionally been left to grow in peace, and game-rich forests in India have enjoyed protection since 300 B.C.

Around the world, the tribes that have lived off the land have invariably been good environmental custodians, leaving their living space more or less intact. But in more densely populated areas, the human hand has gradually altered the landscape on an ever-increasing scale.

Inspired by German visionary Hugo Conwentz, the early conservationists were fascinated by ancient forests. Conwentz believed that it was society's responsibility to maintain valuable habitats in a pristine state for posterity. National parks first saw the light of day in the United States as a concept developed by environmental romantics who wanted future generations to be able to see the landscape in its original state. It took many decades before recreation emerged alongside science as a cornerstone of the conservation movement. Today, we have a range of options – including nature reserve status – for preserving ancient forests like this and their flora and fauna, which here includes red banded polypore, great spotted woodpeckers and horsehair lichen.

By the mid-eighteenth century a new attitude began to emerge in Europe as scientific progress and the principles of the Enlightenment transformed the way people lived through urbanisation and industrialisation. The first successful ascent of Mont Blanc in 1786 marked the birth of mountaineering as a sport. In art, painters began taking an interest in the sublime essence of nature by depicting dramatic landscapes. The educated and affluent took it upon themselves to explore spectacular mountain ranges for aesthetic pleasure, and tourism emerged as a new phenomenon. One by one, the remaining international geographical mysteries were solved, and their discoverers feted as heroes.

As logging intensified in the nineteenth century, some European countries adopted a more protective attitude to their woodlands. In Germany, the Duchy of Bavaria in 1803 purchased an area of forest in Bamberg to protect it from the axe. The forest of Fontainebleau, near Paris, became a centre for outdoor painting, and the Barbizon school of painters, led by Rousseau and Millet, lobbied successfully for the forest to be designated a protected hunting ground in 1858 in honour of its natural beauty. Today, we can regard hunting estates, created by landowners and royalty to encourage an abundance of game beyond the reach of poachers and predators, as harbingers of the national park model. In Sweden, Djurgården – a hunting park close to the centre of Stockholm established by King Johan III in the sixteenth century – is a good example.

In North America, nature preservation took a different tack. The white settlers were strongly influenced by the vast, virgin landscapes that greeted them. Native Americans had lived quietly off the land for generations but the settlers saw potential for endless development and viewed nature as an unlimited resource that could be exploited in the name of economic progress. But as the West was slowly subjugated to the white man's conquests, voices began to grow for some areas to be spared. The artist George Catlin reflected his concern for the welfare of the Indians when he wrote in 1832 that it would be wonderful if America could create a "nation's park" where people and wildlife lived in harmony. This is the first written allusion to the term "national park".

Thirty years later came an important step in this direction when the US government purchased a small part of the Yosemite Valley in California to prevent it from falling into the hands of private developers. Influential policymakers and businessmen at the time wanted people to be able to enjoy the great outdoors and see what America's pristine environment once looked like. It took a few more years for these far-sighted ideas to catch on at political level. The starting gun came in August 1870, when explorers reached a then unknown area called Yellowstone in Wyoming. Astounded by the natural beauty they encountered, the explorers spent their last night round the campfire discussing how to secure its future. Some wanted to privatise Yellowstone and develop tourism; others suggested it be set aside as a national park for the American people. The phrase "national park" was first coined that night. A second expedition party the following year included an artist and a photographer, and their paintings and photographs helped to convince the powers-that-be of Yellowstone's uniqueness. In March 1872, President Ulysses S. Grant signed a decree establishing an area the size of Connecticut and straddling the Yellowstone River as the world's first national park.

This decision was the prelude to modern-day nature conservation, and many people regard the national park idea as one of America's greatest legacies to the world. The concept quickly gained ground in British colonies, where the authorities were concerned about the environmental damage being caused by settlers. The first national parks outside America were a group of three in Canada, including Banff, founded in the 1880s. At about the same time the first national parks were inaugurated in Australia and New Zealand. By the end of the decade, a handful of game reserves had been created in South Africa, while Mexico had also gained its first national park.

In Sweden, the Arctic explorer Adolf Erik Nordenskiöld elaborated on the US concept, writing an article in 1880 in which he compared "nation parks" with works of art. "If people today can pay millions for a picture on canvas or in marble by past masters, what would they not give in a hundred years for a real picture of the motherland as it once was, before farming had yet to shape the landscape, and while there were uncultivated lakeside beaches and forests untouched by the axe." Nordenskiöld's attempts to gain public support for this idea met with little success until 1904, when Professor Hugo Conwentz, a German botanist, visited Sweden and gave a lecture on "dangers threatening the natural landscape ... and proposals for protection". Conwentz, one of Europe's early conservationists, had good connections with researchers at Uppsala University. Among them was Karl Starbäck, a fellow botanist and a member of parliament. A month after Conwentz's lecture, Starbäck submitted a motion to Parliament on the issue. A parliamentary commission was set up and a few years later presented a nature conservancy bill including sections on natural landmarks such as ancient oaks and glacial boulders, along with a set of national park regulations modelled on those in America. In 1909 Parliament voted to establish nine national parks in different parts of the country.

Unlike in the United States, where romantics from different backgrounds joined forces to campaign for national parks, nature conservation in Sweden started off as a scientific domain. However, the men of research paid little heed to how the parks would be managed – a problem that soon became evident at Ängsö National Park, one of the initial group of nine. This archipelago island with its traditional rural landscape went into decline after being left unmanaged, with no grass-cutting or grazing of meadows. Not until the 1930s did the authorities recognise the problem and step in. Other difficulties confronted the great national parks of the mountainous north. Stora Sjöfallet National Park remained untouched for less than a decade before the government announced plans to dam its mighty rivers for hydroelectric power. Conservationists did not protest because they believed the country needed the energy. Back in those days, the goal of protecting national parks as intact wildernesses was conveniently forgotten if it clashed with economic interests. Moreover, there was no organisation in effective charge of Sweden's national parks. The government appointed the Royal Swedish Academy of Sciences' nature conservancy committee to manage the parks and advise ministers, but gave it inadequate resources for the task.

Sweden's extensive right to roam, which gives virtually unlimited access to the nation's countryside, also included national parks. But this unique freedom meant that the national parks remained under-visited because people had so many other areas to choose from. This suited some national park supporters like Rutger Sernander, a botanist who claimed that tourism posed a threat to national park habitats. But such views gradually softened as recreational needs came to the fore in the 1930s, leading for calls to create nature reserves and parks explicitly for leisure purposes. Sten Selander, a well-known literary figure, wrote in 1936 that "it is time for the conservation movement to stress our need for recreation".

Yet conservation values remained in the shadows. By the 1950s, seven new national parks had joined the original group of nine, but they were chosen on an ad hoc basis – sometimes for their specific attributes, sometimes because of the campaigning zeal of certain individuals, and sometimes for both. But conditions changed after World War II, when Sweden's rapid economic growth coincided with a large-scale expansion of the hydropower industry. As dam after dam was built, campaigns began to save the nation's rivers. In 1961 the hydropower industry signed a pact with conservationists that mapped out which rivers could be dammed and which would be preserved for posterity. An immediate fruit of this agreement came a year later with the establishment of Padjelanta National Park – the first new park for twenty years.

The 1960s brought an international conservation revolution – and the wind of change was felt in Sweden too. American author Rachel Carson's book *Silent Spring* focused public attention on pesticides and pollution. A Swedish government report in 1962 led to legislation approving the creation of nature reserves to protect valuable habitats. Nature reserves also serve wider purposes, ranging from preserving small sites of scientific interest to saving the habitats of endangered species and safeguarding popular recreation areas, and account for almost all the areas accorded protection since the 1960s. Sweden currently has around three thousand one hundred of them.

The late 1960s also saw county councils setting up environmental protection units and the formation, in 1967, of the Swedish Environmental Protection Agency, which was later handed responsibility for running national parks. These days, county councils are in charge of day-to-day park management.

The 1970s and 1980s saw intensive efforts to inventory the country's flora and fauna, and the creation of many new nature reserves. A variety of places previously mooted as national parks (Store Mosse, Tiveden and Stenshuvud) were formally inaugurated, after which a more orderly process for national park selection was adopted, with the EPA taking on the role of identifying suitable sites. The current philosophy is that national parks should be large areas that mirror Sweden's physical geography, which is broadly in line with how the International Union for Conservation of Nature (IUCN) defines a national park. New parks

Ten percent of Gotska Sandön was declared a national park in 1909 – a west-facing strip of coastline best known for its stunning sunsets. The Royal Swedish Academy of Sciences argued that the entire island, with its old forests and geological formations, was worthy of protection but faced opposition from the governmental forestry agency, which feared this would restrict pine plantations. Not until 1963 did the entire island gain national park status.

Studies by geographer Axel Hamberg meant Sarek was already well known by the early 1900s and it was his work that led to Sarek being among Sweden's nine inaugural national parks in 1909. The area is invaluable both for science and mountain tourism, and here hikers are shown trekking through Njoatsos-vágge Valley. Together with Padjelanta, Stora Sjöfallet and Muddus national parks, Sarek was recently incorporated in UNESCO's Lapponia world heritage site. Sweden signed the UNESCO world heritage convention in 1984 and has fourteen sites on the list, two of which include national parks (the High Coast and Skuleskogen National Park).

must be at least one thousand hectares in size and enjoy the highest level of formal protection.

One hundred and thirty-five years after first being minted, the national park concept has spread round the world. The official list of national parks kept by the United Nations and IUCN now stretches to almost four thousand – almost a quarter of all protected land worldwide. Conservation mechanisms vary from country to country, both in name and in terms of legal status. We can simply note that just under four percent of the world's one hundred thousand nature protection areas are national parks. And most of them are large areas, in accordance with IUCN guidelines.

A succession of new national parks has been established since the first Swedish plan was adopted in 1989, and in areas and habitats that were formerly under-represented. Some earmarked locations have run into opposition from local people – a common reaction not just in Sweden but internationally too. Nowadays, the authorities in most countries realise the importance of securing local support for new national parks, and in Sweden new management blueprints are being developed at Tyresta, Fulufjället, Kosterhavet and Söderåsen national parks. The Swedish national park centenary has coincided with the publication of a new plan for this unique form of environmental protection – and one that perhaps will help shape the emergence of a new national park model which unites the goals of nature conservation with the aspirations of the people who live nearby.

STENSHUVUD

At dawn a gossamer haze lingers over the rock of Stenshuvud and surrounding countryside. Up here we see with our own eyes the special light that has long drawn artists to this part of Sweden. In good weather, the countryside captivates like a watercolour painting. From the top of the rock our gaze skirts the blue coastline and shimmering horizon as the light clarifies the contours of the land. Sometimes the Danish island of Bornholm is visible in the distance. Below the rocky slope, an open heathland opens up, dotted with green juniper bushes standing like gravestones. The national park's gleaming white sandy beach fades slowly away to the south, where the village of Vik stands in faint outline. Woods dominate to the west, a verdant carpet of leafy trees covering the higher ground.

It is almost one hundred metres down to the sea. We have reached the top of the rock after a short but strenuous walk through the shady beech wood that runs from the visitors' centre. Local people call the rock Stensho, after a giant called Sten who lived with his wife in a cave on the steep north face. The couple are the source of many local fables, including one tale in which two natural stone pillars stand at the entrance to a beautiful garden. This may be a figment of the imagination, but the cave really does exist. Legend has it that skippers who pointed their eyepieces at it were doomed to sink.

The rock has served as an important landmark for seamen since ancient times. "Stenshuvud is a high rock lying tight to the shoreline and serves as a useful point of land for the seafarer," wrote Carl Linnaeus, the renowned Swedish naturalist, in 1749 after visiting the area during his sojourn in Skåne. It has also served as a refuge, and we pass the remains of an ancient settlement built during the Migration Period around 500 A.D. and defended by a now-crumbling stone wall that runs for several hundred metres. Many people sought shelter here during times of war, among them Danish-supporting freedom fighters who battled Swedish troops in the mid-seventeenth century.

Nightfall in Vik and the arched outline of Stenshuvud rises almost one hundred metres above the sea. The rock served as an important landmark for Baltic seafarers down the ages, and the light-house – though no longer needed in the modern age – still shines at its base.

Rugosa roses in flower along the beach. Large thorny beds of the pink flowers grow where the Hollabäckens stream flows into the sea.

Stretching for three kilometres, the sandy beach
becomes a swimmer's para-
dise when onshore winds
take warm currents to the
surface.

German catchfly in bloom on
the summit of Stenshuvud
as a gossamer mist hangs
over the beach. The eastern
precipices are a haunt of
a variety of unusual flower
species, including the rare
black spleenwort and other
localised ferns.

We walk across to the northern summit, from where you can see for miles and follow Hanö Bay as it curves away towards the north-east. The prevailing offshore wind usually makes for a cold sea, but when the wind blows from the Baltic the water temperature can rise sufficiently for a pleasant dip, and then the long beach teems with people.

Standing on the beach allows you to see the rock in its full jutting profile. The top ridge is of harder rock, believed by experts to be relict mountain deposits that have not yet been broken down. This means Stenshuvud has a different geological origin than the horst at Söderåsen National Park to the west, which was forced upwards by underground pressure. Stenshuvud consists of greyish-red porphyry that was once quarried. Stone extraction persisted into the twentieth century, and although the details are sketchy, it is still possible to see evidence of quarrying at the base of the rock where the path heads northwards towards the sea. Walkers also pass Krivaregården, an eighteenth century fishing hut. Eel fishing is an ancient tradition here but prohibited nowadays as the eel is regarded as an endangered species.

We stroll southward along the sandy esplanade between the sea and the alder corridor fringing the beach. The air is still and the sea ebbs and flows gently beside us. A thrush nightingale sings from its perch high in a tree,

The hard bark of the beech tree is usually inhospitable to lichens. But the rock-loving shield lichen has found this trunk on Stenshuvud's south-facing slope to its liking.

Spring colours enliven the heath – an impressive biotope created by an open landscape, grazing animals and nutrient-poor sandy soil. The rounded Trintekull, a bedrock hill, is in the fore-ground.

A beechwood canopy drapes the contours of the land looking north from Stenshuvud. In the background lies Hanö Bay.

Highland cattle graze near Bäckdala in the south of the national park. Keeping the park open through grazing is part of the management plan. Livestock species and breeds vary from year to year.

competing with the distant drone of farm machinery. The beach is impressively long and strangely quiet if you come here at odd times. Stenshuvud is a secluded spot – cordoned off by hills to the west and the sea to the east – and the national park feels surprisingly empty once the visitors have gone home for the day. At three hundred and eighty hectares, it is a small area but nevertheless home to a wide range of habitats and a very diverse flora and fauna.

The light is clear over Hedane, the large open heath in the southern part of the park. Flat as a football pitch, this almost sacred landscape stretches for a kilometre. Here we walk among the many juniper bushes standing solemnly on the dry ground, a perfect habitat for birds like the yellowhammer and northern wheatear. Those with an eye for something more out of the ordinary can look out for common rosefinch and linnet. The flora is interesting, too. Pasqueflower seedpods glitter like miniature Christmas trees in the sharp May sunlight. In late summer, blooming heather turns the heath into a blaze of purple. The rare St Bernard's lily occurs here on the dry sandy earth kept open by grazing sheep, cattle and

horses. Virtually the entire national park is a cultural landscape and even includes an old apple orchard and an arboretum of foreign trees. Some critics suggested the area was too small and disturbed to warrant national park status in 1986, but its exceptional natural beauty and unique ecology spoke firmly in its favour. Beechwoods are the natural vegetation, but have been heavily influenced by Man. Local farmers traditionally kept the area open, and then in the early nineteenth century many trees were felled to make way for fields and hay meadows. Trees were pollarded and coppices grew, and today the national park consists largely of mature beech and hornbeam forest that has developed undisturbed for the last century. Inside the woods we can find the occasional ancient specimen that testifies to an era in which trees stood widely scattered in open countryside.

Hornbeam, an uncommon species elsewhere in Sweden, predominates in some woodland areas. This slender and delicate tree only grows wild in the southernmost part of the country.

A June carpet of wild garlic beside Hollabäcken stream. Wild garlic is uncommon and its pungent onionlike smell permeates the woodland.

DALBY SÖDERSKOG

Beside the small town of Dalby nestles a stately broadleaf wood of old-growth elm, ash and beech. A leafy oasis in a sea of agricultural fields and concrete, insulated from the outside world by dense hazel and hawthorn thickets. Strolling among the tall trees evokes a sense of Southern Europe. In spring, the impression would be very different, with dazzling carpets of spring flowers – wood anemone, hepatica, yellow wood anemone, lesser celandine and corydalis – splashing life and colour beneath the bare trunks. Now, one month on, the leaves have opened and unfurled a cascade of vivid green. Dalby Söderskog feels more like an ancient forest than a managed national park exotic and wild, the nature compels and draws us in. Dog's mercury and ground elder sprout from the fertile blanket of leaf litter covering the rich topsoil.

Walking the neat trails through the chlorophyll-drenched vegetation is a delight, and yet raises a nagging sense of wondering at the back of the mind. After an hour's leisurely walk we have covered the entire national park, and the penny drops. At just thirty-seven hectares, this verdant arbour in central Skåne, in Sweden's far south, is a tiny space – so tiny that "national park" seems an inappropriate description. It feels more like a cultural heritage site rather than a large area "where nature may develop totally undisturbed by cultural influences" – as the Swedish government first defined the national park concept back in 1909. Nine years later, Dalby Söderskog was formally established as a national park.

A former horse paddock and hunting ground, the park has a long and rich history. Intensive forestry in past times has left its mark, and the area would probably qualify as a nature reserve – a more flexible format than a national park – were the authorities considering preservation status today. Not that this detracts from the wood, which impresses with its combination of natural beauty and scientific interest. Although a proposal in 1989 to remove national park status did not go down well at all, Dalby Söderskog is still perhaps best seen as a monument to the nature conservation policies of a bygone age as much as the valuable habitat it is today.

The trail leads the way beneath the beech canopy. The national park hosts mixed deciduous stands of elm, ash and oak: only the beech trees grow unmixed. Man has long left his mark on the wood, but in its current state it is probably wilder than at any time since the Middle Ages.

Spring is an idyllic time at Dalby Söderskog, with hepatica among the many early-blooming flowers.

Elm numbers increased for most of the twentieth century at Dalby Söderskog. The species thrives in shade during its early years and prospers from a denser canopy. Had Dutch elm disease not struck, it would be the dominant tree species today. Many of the national park's elms have succumbed to the disease, first discovered in Sweden in the 1950s. An oak stands in the background.

Seen from Billebjär Hill, Dalby Söderskog is a clearly demarcated grove of trees backed by Romeleåsen Ridge, which rises to one hundred metres above sea level. In early May, when the rapeseed fields bloom, the trees bud at different times. The bare boughs are usually ash, while elm and beech are already in leaf. The highly fertile and calcareous moraine topsoil supports a diverse flora on this southwest-facing slope. (Overleaf.)

According to historical sources, an Augustinian monastery in Dalby used the wood for horse pasture in the sixteenth century, before the Reformation and takeover by the Danish crown. When Skåne came under Swedish sovereignty in 1658, King Charles X Gustav had a stud farm built nearby and the wood once again became a browsing paddock. The stud farm closed in 1703, by which time grazing conditions had deteriorated and oak and beech trees were beginning to encroach. When the stud farm reopened some decades later, the owners built a stone wall round the wood, and by the 19th century the site was less frequently used for horse pasture and had become home to middle-aged stands of oak, beech, ash and elm. After a period of active undergrowth clearance, the wood was left to its own devices until 1880, when ground clearance resumed once more. Thirty four years later, in 1914, the site passed into the ownership of a state-owned forestry company.

From here, the story should be seen in the light of Dalby Söderskog's proximity to Lund University and its prominent natural history professors. In 1904, the Botanical Society of Lund wrote to the Royal Swedish Academy of Sciences asking for the wood to be protected as it was the only natural mixed deciduous forest in the area. Large quantities of timber were felled in 1915 and 1916, after which a coalition of natural history and conservation organisations petitioned the academy for national park status – a proposal approved by Parliament on June 7, 1918. Although the primary motivation was to protect what was regarded as a piece of ancient broadleaf woodland, the authorities nevertheless deemed a management plan necessary to maintain the status quo. Under the supervision of two Lund professors, seventy-five ancient beeches and threatened oaks were cut down a few years later. Periodic felling continued, including the culling of more than one thousand trees (mainly oak and ash) in the early 1960s. Meanwhile, oak has suffered from competition from more shade-tolerant species, causing differences of opinion over how the park is managed. Some people want more proactive measures to promote the growth of oak trees and wild flowers.

The arrival of Dutch elm disease in the late 1980s changed the dynamic once more. In spite of a management plan based on allowing the forest to develop freely, ailing trees were initially removed to curb the spread of disease, and today some areas are more open as a result. But this policy has since been reversed and diseased elms are now left to die and decay. In due course, Dalby Söderskog may indeed become a true old-growth woodland once more, if a little different in character from what its founders intended.

SÖDERÅSEN

From Kopparhatten (Copper Hat), a well known lookout point in Söderåsen National Park, the view is no ordinary Swedish panorama. The leafy forest and dramatic scenery are more reminiscent of continental Europe. We peer down into the deep ravine at Skäralid as it winds and gradually tapers on its journey south and then widens towards a narrow opening in the northeast. Here, the ridge above and the valley below suddenly disappear from view, to be replaced by a forested plain in the distance. The eye travels far in this direction, over a landscape inspiring and exotic in its un-Swedishness. The ravine is several hundred metres wide and almost as deep. Trees that have just acquired the tender green hue unique to a springtime beechwood cloak the valley floor and rocky slopes. Grey patches of overhanging rock, boulders and scree show in the gaps between the trees. Otherwise, the wood is dense and blankets the ridge, its ample green canopy amplifying the ruggedness of the terrain. Behind us, the scenery is more serene – a flat, billowing tableland beneath a stately and inviting forest of beech.

Söderåsen, in the southern province of Skåne, combines the dramatic with the picturesque. And Kopparhatten quickly announces itself as the aesthetic highlight. Söderåsen translates as Southern Ridge but is in fact not a ridge at all but a horst formed when the surrounding land sank into a fault some one hundred and fifty million years ago. The Central European and Scandinavian continental plates collided at this time, creating rift valleys. Skäralid and Nackarpsdalen are two of the three largest and are both found within the national park. Geologically, Söderåsen consists of the oldest gneiss and granite bedrock, while the land that sank into the fault was of much younger clay slate. Or to put it another way, Söderåsen is an Archaean rock hill rising high above the sedimentary bedrock.

Following the Ice Age, plants began colonising the area. Forest grew up on virtually all of what is today the national park. More luxurious woods developed in the ravine, and sparser stands of trees on the thinner soil of the higher plain. Beechwoods thrive in areas with differing nutrient

Burnished autumn colours reflected in the idyllic pond behind the oak tree at Skäralid. A large hotel was built here for tourists in 1906, and almost twenty-five years later the Skärån stream was dammed to create a lake for fishing. Waterfowl like the mallard duck and whooper swan breed in the lake.

Adders occur in the national park, along with a variety of reptiles and amphibians, including the common lizard, grass snake and the moor frog. First and foremost the park is known for the rich insect life in its beechwoods.

The dawn light caresses the wooded ravine at Skäralid. Beech and oak grow on the scree slopes and are joined by ash further down the gorge. Alders thrive in the marshy margins alongside the Skärån stream.

Tinder fungus grows plentifully on beech trees. Ever since the Stone Age, humans have used its crumbly outer layer to make tinder for starting fires. The dense beech canopy casts a heavy shadow over the forest floor, limiting the growth of understorey vegetation.

Banks of mist over Allarp, below Söderåsen, add a new dimension to the view from Kopparhatten on this May morning. (Overleaf.)

levels, and here other broadleaf species occur to differing degrees too. Old-growth deciduous forest dominates at Söderåsen and forms one of the largest expanses of protected broadleaf woodland in Northern Europe. Recreating the natural vegetation that prevailed prior to the arrival of the first humans in these parts is a top priority for the national park authorities, and a major project is underway to restore the area to its former state. This initiative is highly labour-intensive because much of the area was planted with coniferous forest in the last one hundred years or so.

Spruce forests covered significant areas of the park area in previous eras too, but these old-growth trees have since been felled. The management plan envisages returning areas planted with non-indigenous species or subjected to intensive forestry to their original state, which generally means broadleaf woodland. This is a long-term venture aimed at ensuring that people in one hundred years' time can experience Söderåsen as a genuine and diverse primeval-type forest.

Park rangers have felled trees and built high enclosures to promote the growth of broadleaf trees and prevent damage by grazing wild animals. Seedlings have been grown from local stock to ensure the right genetic footprint.

Odensjön Lake lies like an eyeball in the middle of Nackarsdalen Valley. The valley ends in a deep cauldron probably created by glaciers, and experts believe ice has lain here during cold periods both before and after the Ice Age.

Wood violent in bloom beside Skärån stream in springtime. The flora at the base of the ravine is highly diverse and an unusually high number of tree-living moss species occur in the national park.

In all, three hundred hectares of forest land will be restored to its former glory. Though the initiative seems meticulously planned, some critics fear that many uncommon plants and animals that occur in the area today will vanish unless traditional land management techniques are preserved. Others maintain that spruce would have colonised Söderåsen naturally if man had not done the job himself.

Perhaps we should be a cautious about using terms like "primordial" and "pristine" because nature is dynamic and constantly adapting to the changes that shape climate and land use. But the Söderåsen restoration plan reflects an underlying view that recreating the naturally occurring forest has an intrinsic value all of its own. And while the project has made a few waves, most people agree that a long-term approach is necessary in all modern nature conservation efforts.

We take the steep trail from Kopparhatten down into the ravine and follow the Skärån stream. The beechwoods are incomparably clean and tidy, with their airy glades between pillar-like trunks and sparse understorey of dead leaves. The woods up on the ridge have a park-like feel; in the ravine they are harsher. Down here we also find ash and hornbeam among the dominant beech. Skärån is a life-giving artery which collects the water that trickles from the scree slopes.

We follow the watercourse as it twists and turns for seven kilometres until the walls of the ravine start to level out. From here we walk up to Liagården, a small farmstead dating back to the seventeenth century. Clearance cairns and stone fences testify to much older settlements, probably from the late Iron Age. For many hundreds of years – from the Bronze Age to the nineteenth century – local peasants burnt areas of forest to create grazing pasture and fields. Livestock was their main source of income and Söderåsen's forests were gradually converted into pasture, with significant deforestation as a result. For thousands of years the area has seen a complex interplay between the landscape and man's exploitation of its natural resources. The national park can in no way be described as untouched, but it will in time revert to the ancient environment that all national parks are charged with preserving.

The Skärån stream runs into the dam at Skäralid. The clear and clean water is home to the increasingly uncommon brook lamprey. (Previous page.)

The autumnal colour-fest reaches its climax in late October. This is the northern edge of the Söderåsen plain and home to a much wider array of mosses and lichens than the south-facing scree slopes.

Söderåsen's forest and the view from Kopparhatten attract hundreds of thousands of visitors every year. The Skåneleden hiking path passes through the area and a system of marked trails criss-crosses the national park.

STORE MOSSE

Having just climbed the tall, sturdy birdwatching tower south of Lake Kävsjön, I wonder whether the birdsong serenade on this spring evening is the true essence of Store Mosse National Park. The trees are coming into leaf and we are looking out at one of Sweden's best-known lakes for birds, a meeting point for legions of winged creatures. Trumpeting common cranes and the drumming display flights of common snipe fill the air and add a sense of the primeval. These sights and sounds have been played out for tens of thousands of years, with birds returning here spring after spring, long before Store Mosse became a national park. The bond between environment, seasons and animals is near-sacred in a place like this. And it strikes me how important it is to preserve it for future generations.

Or do we come closest to the true soul of Store Mosse (Great Bog) by squelching out into its swampy centre on an autumn day of clear air and heavy silence? We may be in southern Sweden, but nowhere else in this part of the country is the word wilderness more apt than at Store Mosse National Park, with its watery but calming horizon and the dwarf pines perched like bonsai trees on every available tussock. Nature that is beautiful but not quaint.

And there is more. Dark coniferous forests grow in some parts of the national park and airy broadleaf woods in others. Around and about, fragments of cultural landscapes stand isolated on small islets in a sea of fen and marsh, forming a colourless mosaic at this time in early spring before new shoots of green start to show. Store Mosse is nothing if not multifaceted.

A trunk road and a railway line – two transport arteries built long before the park was founded – divide the area in two. We drive south to Lövö, which was settled by crofters in the seventeenth century. These were hardy folk whose farming gradually shaped and changed the surrounding landscape. One hundred years ago, four families lived in this secluded spot in the middle of the bog, where today we find grazing pasture, forest meadows and pollarded trees in an unspoilt paradise that modern visitors can sample by renting one of the old crofters' cottages.

An October frost has turned Lake Kävsjön's withered grass and sedge into pale tendrils. A lone sallow grows alongside a willow bush on the open marsh, formed when the lake's water level fell one metre in 1840 following a drainage operation.

"On still spring evenings one hears the raucous yet sonorous calls of the cranes and the bubbling trills of the curlew," wrote Store Mosse pioneer Edvard Wibeck in a newspaper article in 1936. "Up in the village, people used to predict the weather by listening to the birdcalls and whether they were strongest in east or the west." The national park holds probably the largest breeding population of common cranes in Sweden.

The fields and meadows of Lövö lie on moraine islets in the middle of the bog. Grazing by livestock helps to prevent the land from becoming overgrown. (Previous page.)

Sphagnum dominates the undergrowth in the middle of the bog. Between the tussocks lie shallow hollows which fill with water in spring. These eventually become tussocks, after which heather starts growing, the ground dries out and knotty dwarf pines start sprouting – as here to the north of Södra Svänö.

Store Mosse is the largest bog in Sweden outside Lapland. In the distance, the Småland Hills rise to a height of 200 metres.

A trail leads to Blådöpet, a long and wide triangle of marsh lying in the central part of the bog. We know from our schoolbooks that marshes and bogs are different, and at Blådöpet they lie informatively side by side. Marshes gain most of their moisture from groundwater; bogs from the rain. Bogs grow from the bottom up by peat formation, causing the central areas to bulge upwards. Marshes often form in low-lying areas that attract more nutrient-rich water, and are often covered by forest. Their flora can be highly diverse, as at nearby Björnekullakärret – an easily accessible and exciting site for orchids.

A second trail from Lövö runs north over a slim pine-covered ridge. The ridge is in fact a dune of shifting sand, part of a network that extends throughout the park. Walking along a sand ridge is an enjoyable experience, and the trail wends its way like a narrow causeway across the bog, allowing us to see the full extent of the area and how open it is. The sand is a relic of a former lake from ancient times that covered the low-lying bedrock. Inland ice persisted for a long time in the north of the area, and when the land started to rise around eight thousand years ago it began tipping southward, emptying the lake of water. Exposed to the elements, the sandy bottom dried out and the wind blew the sand into dunes.

The picnic area at Björnakullen is a nice place to watch the sunset in summer. Once the birds have finished their breeding season a heavy silence descends on the area and the bog can feel very empty. (Page 52–53.)

Stone walls built from moraine rocks are characteristic of rural Småland province. This pastoral countryside at Lövö is one of the national park's main highlights. (Previous page.)

The water is as dark as tar out in the middle of the bog. Conservation volunteers have built a walkway so people can see the area at close hand.

The transition to a damper climate a couple of thousand years later saw some of the sandy areas become inundated once again, though the dunes remained intact. Plant colonisation saw northern montane flora gain a foothold alongside southern grassland species, though sphagnum eventually came to dominate. Rotting vegetation slowly turned into peat in the oxygen-deprived wetland, creating the bog as we know it today.

The peat layer is between five and seven metres thick but not until more modern times did local people begin using it as a natural resource. Blocks were cut for fuel and also used to insulate houses. Relics of peat extraction at Kittlakull and Horssjön, both inside the national park, can still be seen – and indeed peat extraction continued until the middle of the last century. And therein lies a paradox, for while Store Mosse is seen as a wilderness icon for southern Sweden, it bears numerous marks of human activity. Archaeological finds have revealed a human presence in the area as long ago as the Stone Age, when the inland ice was still retreating. The nineteenth century saw the drainage of Lakes Kävsjön and Horssjön as part of a largely unsuccessful attempt to create new arable land. Also, the park's forests have been cut for timber at regular intervals. Fortunately, the open bogs have retained most of their original character and are the main reason the area is a national park today.

Store Mosse shares much in common with Muddus National Park. The two are almost as far apart as it is possible to be in Sweden, but both have very large bogs and are well known internationally, having received the European Council Diploma of Protected Areas. Store Mosse is a Ramsar Convention wetland of international importance, while Muddus is part of Unesco's Laponian Area, a world heritage site. The two also share a link to Edvard Wibeck, a nature conservancy pioneer and early natural history photographer. During his long life, Wibeck (who died in 1972 at the grand old age of ninety-five) focused public attention on the biological merits of both national parks and was as such their originator. Muddus National Park was certainly his creation, and way back in 1905 he advocated protection for Lake Kävsjön – a recommendation that bore fruit twenty years later. Despite advancing years, Wibeck remained sprightly and campaigned in the 1950s for Lake Kävsjön's protected status to be extended to the whole of Store Mosse. This took just as long to achieve, and it was not until a year after his death that his wish was granted when Store Mosse became a nature reserve. A further eleven years later, Store Mosse became southern Sweden's largest national park.

NORRA KVILL

A steep path follows the lonely forest road up to Stora Idgölen Mere. We pick our way along the stream, past uprooted trees and fallen trunks, and on reaching the miniature lake are greeted by Sweden's most inviting old-growth coniferous forest – Norra Kvill National Park. The path winds along the bank, past the reflections of the trees in the still water, and disappears into the woods. This is a special place and unlike any other of Sweden's national park forests. Standing bolt upright in a thick carpet of green moss, the trees are slim and almost scrawny, with no gnarled or chunky trunks to betray their true age. The ground is an obstacle course of sturdy boulders and fallen logs. A host of holes and hollows lie concealed beneath the moss, ready to swallow any unwary footstep. The fallen trees – spruces and pines freely interspersed – resemble the masts of sailing ships, brought down by age and wind. The rich green layer of stair-step moss carpeting the boulders and rotting logs creates a fairytale atmosphere, and you can almost imagine the presence of magical beings hiding among the trees.

It takes centuries for moss to grow into thick carpets. Here, the moss and the spire-like trees indicate that saws and axes have not been seen at Norra Kvill for a very long time. Many of the pines are more than three hundred and fifty years old, which also suggests that the area has long been spared from forest fires. Indeed, scientific analysis has shown that the oldest trees have not been exposed to fire for several centuries. Going further back, however, forest fires occurred every twenty years or so (an unusually high frequency) from the early fifteenth to the late seventeenth century. The abrupt end to this cycle was probably because the crofters who moved into the area after this date extinguished the fires to preserve their homes and livelihoods. This changed the composition of the woods, benefiting spruce, and the local flora and fauna. The only fire known to have occurred at Norra Kvill in modern times was a small blaze a century ago in the north-west of the park, where the trees are much younger.

Once we have found our way to the national park, hidden away in rural Småland, it is easy to share the enthusiasm of Daniel Frykman, the man

Unusually large swathes of stair-step moss cover logs and rocks on the forest floor at Norra Kvill National Park. Two small lagoons are found in the park, and here we glimpse Stora Idgölen Mere from the east.

A goldeneye on Stora Idgölen Mere. This duck probably breeds here in some years, alongside other species like common teal and mallard.

Large amounts of deadwood lie on the slopes of Idhöjden Hill, two hundred and forty metres above sea level. The oldest living pines have stood for around three hundred years. The hill stands on the edge of the Småland Highlands, close to the border with Östergötland county.

who did most to have the area designated a national park. Like a number of counterparts who helped to found other national parks, Frykman was a forester and in charge of managing Norra Kvill. The pristine nature of the area fascinated him and in 1925 he formally proposed that it be designated a national park. The Royal Swedish Academy of Sciences supported his recommendation, noting a need for Sweden to offer increased protection to the few untouched forests remaining in the south of the country. Though far-sighted, this idea was not fully reflected in the government's decision, in 1927, to confer national park status: only twenty-seven hectares of old-growth forest on state-owned land were included in the proposed park. Clearly, the policymakers of the day thought logging income more important than nature conservation. Norra Kvill's small size meant it fell outside the national park definition adopted subsequently by the International Union for Conservation of Nature. Just over half a century later, in the late 1980s, the Swedish Environmental Protection Agency proposed more than tripling the park's size as part of a country-wide plan for Sweden's national parks. The agency argued that the plan would make Norra Kvill more of an entity, even if it still fell short of international norms. Idhöjden Hill and Lilla Idgölen Mere were both included within the park boundaries.

The park may be small in stature, but as a symbol for ancient forest it

has few equals. We walk to the vantage point on the top of the hill, two hundred and thirty metres above sea level, from where grandiose wood-covered ridges stretch for miles. These hilly, forested tracts of northern Småland province are sparsely populated and reminiscent of Sweden's empty mountain uplands. The difference between the park's lowest and highest points is sixty metres. After walking through this countryside for a few hours you feel it in your legs. Pine is the dominant tree species, but impressive spruces grow in the damper depressions. Though younger than the oldest pines, they have thicker trunks with a circumference of up to two-and-a-half metres and are thirty-five metres tall.

It is a little surprising to find deciduous species like elm, ash and linden scattered among the spruces. These trees are found in a lush but near-impenetrable small ravine through which the stream from Stora Idgölen Mere runs, at times concealed by rocks and boulders. In summer, the mere is largely covered by water lilies. The park's flora is surprisingly diverse, especially in the spruce stands, and pasqueflowers grow on the meagre pine-covered soil. A wide range of mosses and lichens occur in the park, along with numerous animal and bird species. These include bats, which favour hollow tree trunks, and lucanid beetles, which thrive on dead logs and whose presence is a strong indicator of the park's biological value.

Spire-like pines reflected in the calm waters of Stora Idgölen Mere, where a caraway plant has found an unlikely foothold on an island tussock.

A frosty night has frozen the surface of Stora Idgölen Mere. The small lake is home to several species of sphagnum, which come in a range of different colours – yellow, brown, green and red (the latter known as *Sphagnum magellanicum*) – and turn white when they dry.

Weakened by red banded polypore, a parasitic mushroom that causes rotting, these large spruces have fallen beside the trail through the national park.

BLÅ JUNGFRUN

From the mainland, Blå Jungfrun appears as a bulge on the horizon – an alluring shape in the Kalmar Sound that brings Carl Linnaeus to mind. Recording his travels on the islands of Öland and Gotland in 1745, the celebrated naturalist wrote, "…if any place in the world looks frightful, this is certainly amongst the grimmest." Nowadays we see nature differently. Blå Jungfrun is a national park because of its beauty and unusual form. No one calls it frightful; but inaccessible it certainly is.

We approach the island by ferryboat and watch as the bump in the sea slowly rises to a high dome while becoming reddish in colour (not blue as the name Blå Jungfrun, or Blue Virgin, might have us believe). The boat moors where the smooth cliff-face plunges into the sea. If conditions permit, visitors can disembark at Sikhamn harbour, but sometimes other more sheltered spots are required. In the sunshine, Blå Jungfrun is a welcoming island. First to greet us are the flat rocks. Bare rock dominates, its surface pleasant to the touch and offering good friction for walkers. Wonderful cliffs curve, as if sculpted, towards the sea: hard rock and soft contours are an exquisite combination. Perforating the rock are cavities of different shapes and sizes, known geologically as giants cauldrons. The island is like a huge hump. In the north the push side is evenly rounded, where the smoothing pressure of the inland ice was greatest. In the south, the dome slopes towards a sharp precipice. This is the leeward side, where the ice cut into the rock rather than smoothing it. The gradient was flatter and the boulders, shunted aside, accumulated on the beach. The waves have kneaded and pounded the rock since the Ice Age, especially along the shoreline. The Stensliperiet (Rock Polisher) in the southwest is nature's own artist's workshop, with large round pebbles in all sorts of colours.

We look up at the sparse pinewood on the island's highest point, precisely eighty six metres above sea level – our destination. The anticlockwise walk round the island reveals the national park in a nutshell. At one thousand, one hundred and fifty metres in length and eight hundred and forty metres wide, the island is not big. Yet the trail is demanding,

The rocks at Sikhamn have been polished smooth by the sea. Blå Jungfrun was once believed to be a meeting place for Sweden's witches and was known as Blåkulla, named after the German mountain Blocksberg. Legend had it that the Devil spent time here and the witches flew in on their broomsticks.

Black guillemots used to be the island's commonest bird but the cormorant has since usurped that role. Cormorants are controversial as they compete with fishermen for their prey and live in colonies that kill trees and underlying vegetation with their droppings. They occur in large numbers on Blå Jungfrun but do not breed.

The jungle-like deciduous woods in the south contain a variety of high-grade species. Linnaeus discovered that ivy grew plentifully, but this creeper has disappeared in recent times due to a series of cold winters.

Mirage-like in the early dawn light, Blå Jungfrun inspires the imagination. It is said that seafarers had places of sacrifice on the island long before the medieval era. In 1896, the writer Verner von Heidenstam got married here. "It was the most terrible place I could obtain hurriedly as the island is regarded as an old seat of Satan, where people usually cannot even set foot," he said.

and we walk across the flat rocks to the southern end, where a brushy oak forest grows, interspersed with aspen, lime and rowan trees. The oldest are several hundred years old and were covered in ivy until the introduction of rabbits in the mid-nineteenth century. The rabbits took a heavy toll on the ivy but died out during the cold winters of the 1940s, allowing the ivy to recover only to disappear again due to cold winters. A rich flora includes sweet woodruff and coralroot bittercress. Higher up, the slope becomes precipitous and the railings drilled into the rock offer a welcome helping hand. You don't willingly stray from the path here. We climb higher through the different vegetation zones, from broadleaf woodland to the pine trees that share the crest with stunted birch trees. The view to the south is panoramic and the eye penetrates deep into the Kalmar Sound, with the island of Öland to the left and the mainland on the right. The vista reflects our notion of Blå Jungfrun as a high and isolated cliff in the sea.

"On this rock, at certain times of year, it is said that Nordic witches hold meetings to test their arts and signs," wrote the Swedish ecclesiastic and author Olaus Magnus in 1555. He described the island as Jungfrun (Virgin), the name apparently used by seafarers "to avoid bad omens and storms at sea". Linnaeus also mentioned the old legends, referring to the island of Blåkulla between the mainland and Öland.

Blåkulla translates as Blockula and was a mythical meadow which the devil would attend during a witches' Sabbath. The belief that Blå Jungfrun was the site of Blockula existed already in the fifteenth century.

The island has never been settled due to its inhospitable terrain and exposed position. In olden times, sailors would do their utmost to avoid setting foot on land and there are stories of how taking a stone with you from Blå Jungfrun would bring endless bad luck until it was returned to the island. National park rules now prohibit the removal of any stone or rock, but quarrying took place here in the early twentieth century and stone cutters were an everyday sight until the island became a national park. The stone cutters were responsible for blasting open one of the island's giants cauldrons and also built a few cottages in the oakwoods and cut down areas of forest for firewood. Remains of the three quarries can be seen by the southern beach today.

Karl Starbäck, a nature conservancy pioneer, campaigned against the development of the island and vainly attempted to persuade Parliament to declare it a national park. Quarrying resumed following World War I, after which financier Torsten Kreuger purchased the island and donated it to the state. In 1926, the government finally granted it national park status.

Rapakivi granite glows in the dawn light at Lervikshamn harbour. This rock is 1.4 billion years old and takes its ruddy colour from the mineral potash feldspar. The island is an isolated relict mountain standing on the seabed. Bare flat rocks cover two thirds of it. (Previous page.)

Plants grow only where earth has accumulated in the cracks between the rocks, but lichens proliferate on the stony ground and trees. More than two hundred different lichen species have been recorded.

Visitors sometimes have to take a small boat from the ferry to disembark and tourists may only visit during daytime.

KOSTERHAVET

A profusion of islets and skerries dots the sea around Koster on Sweden's west coast. The smooth grey bedrock islands of this archipelago rise naked from a clear sea more saline and biologically diverse than anywhere else in Swedish territorial waters. A gale force wind from the Skagerrak whips the waves into frothing white tops, drenching the outer skerries in spray. From our vantage point at Arnholmen we feel small in the midst of nature's power. Pelagic seabirds rarely seen in these parts are sometimes driven within sight of land by autumn storms. Though this is a wet and miserable summer's day, it is always magnificent and compelling to witness nature's power. The landscape before us has definite parallels to the larger archipelagos of the east coast, and yet has an essence all of its own. Sea and land have different ways of converging, and the contours of the land play a defining role at Kosterhavet. The islands are chubby and high, creating a rocky landscape like no other Swedish archipelago I have visited.

Through the drizzle and spray we can just make out two lighthouses, standing exposed to the full force of the wind on the crest of Yttre Ursholmen, a small islet four kilometres to the south. The archipelago has been shaped by the hand of man ever since ancient times and none of the islands have gone untouched. But for the harbour seals that have found a haven on the islets between Ursholmarna and Sydkoster this is of no consequence. Indeed, their colony is the largest on the west coast.

Kosterhavet and its marine environment and islands are the only national park on the west coast and Sweden's first and only marine national park. The protected zone covers a wide area and includes the cluster of islets and skerries we have visited. The two main islands, Nordkoster and Sydkoster, are both inhabited and serve as human enclaves in the centre of this maritime refuge, though only the islands' beachside areas are included in the park itself.

Nordkoster is largely barren, with attractive pebble beaches; Sydkoster is a more vibrant place of deciduous woods and agricultural fields. The

Rain clouds loom over Yttre Ursholmen, Sweden's most westerly island with buildings. Three families lived here for seventy years after the two lighthouses were built in 1891, the first in Sweden to be made from concrete. The forest in the foreground lies beneath Sydkoster's highest point, Valfjället, which stands fifty-nine metres above sea level.

A red fox ambles along a Sydkoster beach looking for food. The national park is an important refuge for marine and coastal animals and plants. Many species of waterfowl occur here, while the larger islands are home to mammals such as the blue hare.

Sea holly, known locally as "Koster thistle", is nationally rare but grows commonly on Kosterhavet's beaches. The soil and climate supports a highly diverse flora: close to six hundred different plant species have been recorded, an exceptionally high number for such a small area.

Colonies of harbour seals breed to the south of the Koster islands and around the Ursholmarna islands. The seals are excellent divers and can spend long periods under water. In 1988 a viral infection decimated the seal population on Sweden's west coast, since when the illness has recurred in bouts.

narrow sound between them is a popular navigation channel for boat traffic. Cottages and cabins line the shoreline, as befits a prime fishing district. Ramsö, another inhabited island a bit further south, is outside the marine park. Abutting it to the east are a string of small pearls like Kockholmen, a wooded peninsula that has the potential over time to develop into a virgin-type coastal forest.

Marine and aquatic environments cover around ninety percent of the park, which extends from Kosterfjorden in the east a fair way out into the Skagerrak and then continues south for thirty kilometres or so perpendicular to the coast. The northern tip is adjacent to Norway's Hvaler Marine National Park and the two represent a shining example of modern cross-border environmental cooperation. Both parks were conceived and developed in parallel and formally opened in 2009 – exactly one hundred years after the first Swedish and European national parks saw the light of day.

Bare islets, rocky beaches and shallow bays – a coastal landscape unmatched anywhere in Sweden – form the visible part of the national park. But most of the protected zone is hidden from sight: a rich undersea environment that is home to five thousand species of marine animal and plant, two hundred of them found nowhere else in Sweden. The Kosterfjord shelf, at a depth of two hundred and fifty metres between the archipelago and the mainland, is saline, cold and an ocean-like environment. Eighty five metres below the surface lies Sweden's only coral reef. Built by the deep-water *Lophelia pertusa* coral, this cold-water reef almost matches the

biodiversity of its tropical counterparts and is home to numerous highly specialised organisms. The creatures present also vary between different habitats, such as rock faces and sandy bottoms, while the shallow bays around the islands are precious biotopes for species like kelp, which grows here in dense forests.

Kosterhavet can be seen as a giant experiment in nature conservation. Protecting and conserving marine environments is always a challenge. Strong underwater currents feed the area, and preventing pollution and invasive species from entering the protected zone is almost impossible. The national park is also a home and workplace for many people, and hunting and fishing has been a natural part of life here down the ages. Kosterhavet's elevation to national park status has seen new rules drawn up in consultation with local people. These allow fisheries and hunting to continue in the marine park but under stricter conditions than in the past. Tourism is a major industry and it, too, has gained a new framework to reflect the standing and attention that goes with being a national park. The hope now is that the park can act as a catalyst to promote long-term sustainable development in this unique and special coastal area.

Heather in bloom at Ramnefjäll on Sydkoster, whose coastal meadows are just one of Kosterhavet's many natural habitats. The scenery has varied historically from open ground to woodland. The brushy pine forest on the main islands was planted fifty years ago. Most of Nordkoster and Sydkoster islands, with their population of two hundred and seventy people, are outside the national park boundaries.

A sunbeam illuminates a strip of sea at Hästholmen. Here, lichens grow on the bare rock and wild flowers sprout from the crevices.

Fifteen metres under the sea, plankton cast a green sheen over an underwater rockface. The rocks provide a haven for many North Sea species, including white and orange alcyonaria, starfish and bryozoa. Wrasse species, like goldsinny to the left and cuckoo wrasse to the right, find food and shelter among the rocks.

A lion's mane jellyfish floats above the kelp and shellfish beds of the Koster islands. The oxygen-rich waters have the salinity of an ocean.

Knotted wrack and bladder wrack seaweed grow close to the surface, while pine trees fringe the Nordkoster shore-line. The Koster islands are unusually wooded in comparison with Sweden's other west coast archipelagos.

The jet-black diabase rock at Yttre Ursholmen is igneous rock derived from magma that once forced its way through cracks in the gneiss bedrock. Diabase is rich in iron and looks like streaks of asphalt from a distance. Some seven hundred diabase dykes have been counted in the Koster archipelago and a disused diabase quarry is found on the island of Inre Ursholmen. (Overleaf.)

Depending on the weather, the coast can range from a tranquil paradise to a raging inferno. Here, a January storm whips the sea off Nordkoster into a frenzy of waves and spray. The high seas on this particular day forced the cancellation of all ferry services to and from the island.

The name Koster is thought to come from "kostir", an Old Norse word meaning eating place, probably in reference to the excellent fishing off the islands. Picturesque fishing shacks like these at Långevik on Sydkoster dot the coastline.

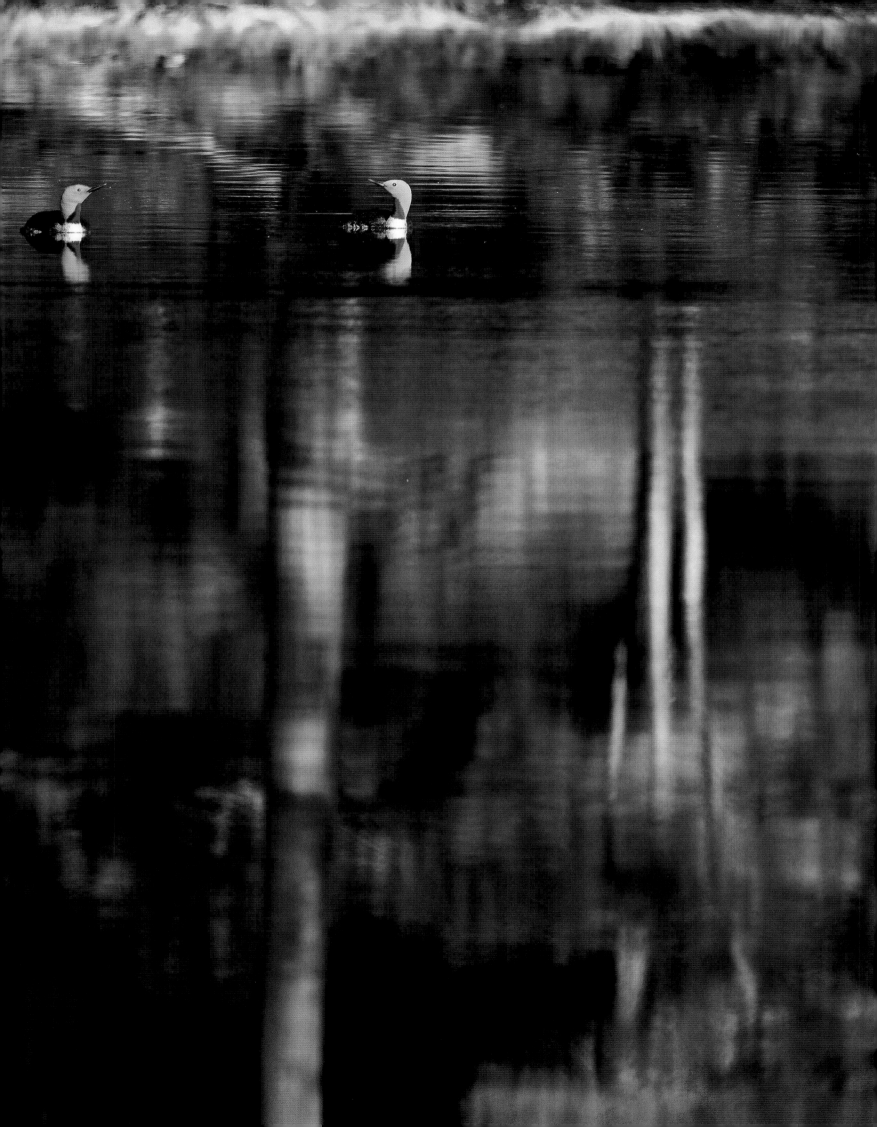

TRESTICKLAN

Trestickel means trident in English and is an apt description for Lake Stora Tresticklan. This inaccessible lake, deep in the forests of Dalsland along Sweden's border with Norway, has several finger-like promontories that jut out from the shore to create a trident or fork-like shape. Just as other small lakes in this often forgotten national park, Lake Stora Tresticklan is lobe-shaped due to the nature of the local bedrock. The peaks of this undulating forest wilderness run along long ridges from north to south, sometimes stretching for kilometres. In the valleys between them lie lakes and mires, sometimes as far as fifty metres down. Seen from the sky, the regularly spaced ridges look like the ribs of a gigantic washboard. The bedrock at Tresticklan National Park is ancient and acidic veined gneiss, which is unfavourable to plant life but hard enough to withstand erosion. In the depressions between the ridges geologists have found softer rock types that have been weathered down, but because the park area was not covered by the sea after the last Ice Age (it is too high up) the depressions did not fill with earth and moraine to level out the land. This is why flat-rock areas extend so widely at Tresticklan.

The national park is impressive and the largest uninhabited and roadless area of wilderness in southern Sweden. It reveals some of its secrets during a hike to Orshöjden, the highest point in the park at two hundred and seventy-five metres. We start at the national park entrance, deserted today, from where the forest follows the contours of the ribbed landscape like a kind of green rollercoaster. The walking is strenuous when you have to march up and down the ridges at perpendiculars; following them longitudinally is a whole lot easier. The landscape is barren, with well spaced pines that are unexpectedly similar in size and stature. So much so that they almost look as if they were planted simultaneously, but this is not the case and in other respects the forest certainly looks pristine. Though by no means large, the pines are between one hundred and one hundred and fifty years old – a respectable age. Their symmetry is due to major forest fires in the mid-nineteenth century, which destroyed the old forest and paved the way for

A pair of red-throated loons early one May morning at Hälletjärn Mere, deep inside Tresticklan National Park. These birds often breed in small pools with no or very few fish and must fly long distances – sometimes twenty kilometres or more – to suitable fishing lakes.

Wildlife is thinly spread over the barren terrain of the park, though roe deer occur widely. Bird species include nightjar, capercaillie, hazelhen and several species of wood-pecker and tit.

The national park is home to a pack of wolves that ranges freely across the Swedish-Norwegian border. The entire wolf population in both countries is descended from three wolves that crossed over from Finland in the late 1970s.

The rib-like series of ridges creates a drainage flow from north to south. This stream at Skacklenäset feeds Lake Stora Tresticklan.

Hälletjärn Mere lies in a joint valley in the northern part of the park. Around eighty forest lakes are found in the area. (Overleaf.)

an entirely new generation. No large-scale logging has ever been carried out. Mires and flat-rocks cover nearly half the park and serve as effective barriers to modern forestry. The lie of the land and its barren soil is also a factor in why the trees are modest in size.

The eye travels far through these airy wooded vaults as the trail leads us farther and farther from human habitation. After hiking for a kilometre or so we reach Lilla Tresticklan, a long and narrow forest lake. The water level in it and its larger neighbour Lake Stora Tresticklan have been controlled dating back before the area became a national park, and the plan is to reduce it in the future.

We hike on to Orshöjden in the heart of the park. After climbing a steep slope we arrive at the top of the domed ridge. The crest stretches for several kilometres and between the trees we glimpse a sliver of the well-known Lake Stora Le to the east. Behind the trees on to the west, the crumpled terrain sweeps away in a seemingly endless swathe of forest towards the Norwegian border. There are no vantage points to offer a panoramic view, but the sheer size of the area is evident anyway. As the crow flies, it is three kilometres to the nearest forest track and a good deal farther to the nearest house. Nowhere else in southern Sweden do we get closer to a true forest wilderness.

Red-throated loons resting on Hälletjärn Mere as the morning sunlight reflects the surrounding pine forest on the water's surface.

Small captivating pools and meres nestling in the forest are typical of Tresticklan National Park. Most of the trees have narrow trunks and include a high proportion of dead and decaying wood, though some old-growth trees more than two hundred years old can also be found. The sparse ground vegetation reflects the barren nature of the land.

Isolated and uninhabited as the national park is, it is not without a human history. Down the ages Tresticklan has served as a hiding place for robbers, the soldiers of Charles XII, and Norwegian resistance fighters in World War II. An old highway to the Norwegian town of Halden, south of Oslo, passed through the area via a wooden footbridge at Lake Stora Tresticklan used by villagers from Rävmarken when they travelled to the Norwegian market.

The forest was also a part-time home to Orre-Bryngel, a mysterious hunter who lived in a cave on Orshöjden when on fishing expeditions. He dressed as a trapper in greatcoat, goatskin boots and a cap made from a loon pelt, carrying knives, two pistols and a powder horn in his belt.

Below Orshöjden lies Bråtarne, a former settlement of which remains only the foundations of a house and a clearing in the forest. People lived here from around 1730 until 1904. One of the men from Bråtarne mined iron ore deposits in the area and built a forge at Sminäset on one of Lake Stora Tresticklan's promontories.

DJURÖ

Djurö National Park is the ultimate Swedish hideaway: no group of islands is farther from land than this collection of islets clustered in the middle of the Lake Vänern. To get there we must take the park superintendent's boat as no scheduled services operate. The water is choppy in the gale-force wind and our boat pitches and tosses on the waves. Vänern is Europe's third largest lake, so vast that in many ways it is more like an inland sea – and its waters can be treacherous.

But for all its great size, Lake Vänern feels somehow more manageable than the open sea, with a horizon that is finite rather than endless. The boat tumbles forward over the waves. The environment looks maritime but this is freshwater, and the half-expected smell of salt carried on the spray never comes. Instead, the air is filled with a fresh sweetness that tells us the water is drinkable, while the waves breaking on the beach have a burnished bronze sheen. Lake Vänern combines the unsullied water of an inland waterway with the power and force of the ocean.

The national park encompasses the underwater environment as well as the thirty-five islets – and equal number of skerries and rocks – of the Djurö archipelago. We disembark on Djurö itself to explore this remote island landscape. The feeling of isolation descends immediately at the old hunting lodge tucked away in a sea of reeds in the adjacent bay. Lake Vänern's immensity has receded, and we are left with only the whistling of the wind to remind us of our seclusion. Back in medieval times, a widow and her two sons moved out here during a period of popular uprisings in King Gustav Vasa's reign. A century or so later another group of people arrived and settled in the same spot. Eventually they bought the land and eked out a living from fishing and small-scale farming. Domestic animals arrived. In time, up to three families were living on Djurö, making lengthy and risky rowing trips to the market towns of Mariestad and Lidköping to sell freshly caught fish. Properties were handed down from father to son through the generations until 1890, when the forest-owning Kempe family bought the islands and turned them into a hunting estate. Attracted by the

The eastern side of the Djurö archipelago is a place of stony beaches and flat rocks. Among the pebbles of Danska Holmen grow common skullcap, tufted vetch and orpine, once used to allay fevers.

Fallow deer were introduced as game in 1912 by the Kempe brothers and a small herd of twenty or so animals still survives. Though restricted to the main island, they are strong swimmers and capable of making it across to the other islets.

Built in 1912, the lighthouse on Malbergsholmen is no longer in use. The lighthouse on the main island dates back to 1872. Ships up to eighty-eight metres long and thirteen metres wide use the channel that passes the archipelago.

In strong westerlies, the waves pound against the gneiss rocks on Djurö's western shore. A seventy-metre shelf lies beneath the lake just offshore from here. Lake Vänern holds thirty percent of all Sweden's freshwater.

isolated location, they introduced roe, fallow and red deer on Djurö, along with grouse, pheasant and hare, to provide adequate game for well-to-do hunting parties.

One might imagine that Djurö (Animal Island) gained its name during the Kempe family's era. In fact, it dates back many centuries and is rather a contradiction as historically only a few mammal species inhabited the island, even if Djurö was a haven for amphibians, lizards, snakes and waterfowl. Overgrazing by deer gradually had a negative impact on the island's plant and tree life, and a heavy cull took place when the islands became a national park. Today, around twenty fallow deer still survive on the main island and we catch glimpses of them scampering off through the foliage as we explore on foot.

By the end of my walk round the island I find myself revelling in the nature and the special atmosphere of this remote location. Sparse pine forest dominates, with tall old trees intermingled with bonsai-like dwarves standing against a decorative backdrop of bilberry sprigs and heather. Some areas are almost like a Japanese garden. Logging took place here until the 1940s, since when the woods have been left to grow free from

woodcutters and their machinery. The forest is slowly returning to its former glory and in some areas is primeval-like, with storm-blown and decaying logs lying on the ground. The western shore offers up a little coastal drama, as waves whipped by the strong wind pound heavily against the rocks. In the far distance the Värmlandsnäs peninsula is just visible as a thin tongue of land protruding above the water. Looking northwards towards the horizon is an aesthetic pleasure. In many ways it bears all the hallmarks of the archetypal Swedish archipelago: flat-rocks polished smooth by the retreating ice, bare rocks and pine-clad islets, reefs in the channels and reedbeds fringing the bays. If transplanted to the Baltic coast these islands would look perfectly at home. But lying here, in the middle of Sweden's inland sea, they are special and "in an exclusive location", to quote the nature conservation brochure.

We reach the other islands by kayak. The southernmost of them, Gisslan, is especially interesting due to its chalky soil, which supports a richer flora than the other islands. A dense grove of old linden trees grows in the centre. The rock on the northern side of Djurö contains several

Distant thunder clouds moving north over Vänern. The Värmlandsnäs peninsula is just visible on the horizon, at least eight kilometres away across the open water.

The Djurö hunting lodge was built a century ago in the place farmed by the island's original settlers in the 1700s and 1800s. The lodge served as overnight quarters for well-do-do gentlemen who came here to hunt deer and other game.

Heather grows plentifully in the low pine forest along Djurö's western shore.

This tiny rocky marsh on Danska Holmen is home to a miniature garden of wild flowers, including orpine, St. John's wort and golden rod. In the distance lies Kinnekulle, a ridge on the mainland which rises to a height of two hundred and sixty metres.

layers of greenstone, whose alkaline properties also benefit plant life. On the western side, the rocks form a steep edge to the shoreline. The eastern side is completely different, its flat-rocks dotted with small marshy areas and sloping gently down to the water's edge. Some of the small naked islets offshore boast brightly coloured flowers growing in crevices: purple loosestrife, orpine and St. John's wort. From the eastern side of the archipelago we can observe Kinnekulle, a hill on the mainland whose attractive symmetrical profile is visible twenty-five kilometres out into the lake. None of these low-lying islets stands higher than twenty metres above the water.

We paddle our kayaks into a bay and lie down to rest on one of the rocks, warm from the rays of the sun, and scoop up some of the crystal-clear water to drink. What freedom and luxury! Lake Vänern is a water catchment area and the water itself so pure it can be drunk straight from the lake. A magnificent white-tailed sea eagle, a bird that has returned to Djurö in recent years, drifts over as if to reinforce the untouched essence of this faraway island refuge.

TIVEDEN

The trail to Lake Trollkyrkesjön winds over a ridge of erect pine trees and leads into the heart of Tiveden National Park. The dense overhead canopy restricts the sky to faint patches of light, but one can see surprisingly far at eye-level through the trees. Reindeer moss grows in tangled carpets alongside the rocky path, which soon enters a sharp descent. Walking in this rolling terrain of rocks and trees is a strenuous business.

The forest closes in. Spruce trees stand shoulder to shoulder with pines growing in the hollows, and slabs of rock give way to earth and gnarled roots. Below, the lake shimmers through the trees, like an eye shining in its socket. The water is dark, yet paler than the murky forest. The trees thin out and we reach the lakeside, where the canopy parts and the sky opens up. The aroma of bog myrtle fills the air and speeding clouds are reflected in the still water as they scud past above a silent curtain of silhouetted trees. Peaceful and inviting, Lake Trollkyrkesjön is one of thirty or so lakes at Tiveden – islands of water that have a natural attraction for hikers and animals alike.

Tiveden and its mighty forest is a truly magnificent setting. "Located near the heart of southern Sweden, the national park is a large tract of evergreen forest with deep fissure valleys, chaotic expanses of huge boulders, and a powerful sense of wilderness," says the tourist brochure. But what makes the area so untamed and special? The high density of very old trees is one factor. The thick spruce and pine trunks and numerous decaying logs that lie scattered about testify to the forest's great age, while the green moss cloaking the rocks and tree-stumps lends a sense of benign neglect – of a place left to its fate.

These hallmarks are all typical of ancient forest and can be found in other national parks, too. But Tiveden has a character all of its own. This rolling landscape of huge boulders, hills and depressions, where small meres and marshes nestle has an air of unbending natural power. Plant life is sparse beneath the dense overhead cover but we still note a degree of variation as we walk among the trees. Tiveden may look

A gentle mist enhances the magic of Tiveden on the trail leading to Stenkälla. Large boulders lie scattered among the undulating granite ridges. Logging has occurred at Tiveden in the past, but after a major fire in 1835 the area has remained relatively untouched and been spared the intensive forestry seen in many other parts of Sweden. The oldest trees are more than three hundred years old.

The fauna is fairly standard coniferous-forest fare but does include an unusually high number of beetle species and a large capercaillie population.

Winter is about to release its icy grip on Lake Trollkyrke-sjön, which lies close to the centre of the national park. Overlooking the lake is Troll-kyrka (Troll Church), a rocky hillock thought to have been a place of sacrifice in pagan times. Outdoor free-church meetings were held here during a major religious revival in the nineteenth century.

The rock of Junker the Hunter is a magnificent column of rock once deposited here by retreating glaciers. Located just outside the original park border, it is due to become part of the national park when a further seven hundred hectares of forest are added to Tiveden's protected zone.

uniform at first sight, but scratch the surface and its variety and nuances are striking.

The forest here is a true wilderness and reminds me of the old sagas about trolls and little creatures that dwelled amongst logs and rocks. It is no coincidence that John Bauer, a well-known Swedish fairy tale illustrator, lived in these parts. The most famous site in the national park is Stenkälla, where people went to make sacrifices to the spirits in pagan times and which overlooks a valley with a small lake. Within a few minutes later we have reached Trolltiven, the most suggestive place in the park and legendary home of Tyr, the Norse god of war and victory. Giant boulders once carried and dumped here by retreating glaciers are scattered all around. Beneath some of them lie mysterious cave-like cavities with damp walls. Seen through the forest half-light, the mightiest of Stenkälla's boulders conjures up the imagination when seen in profile. More impressive still is the rock of Junker the Hunter, a mighty twenty-metre column of stone close to Lake Trehörningen. According to medieval legend, Junker sought to marry a fair maiden from the Sverker family — against her father's wishes. The two lovers eloped to Tiveden along with

Dawn at Lake Trehörningen in the month of May. This tranquil haven appealed to writer Verner von Heidenstam, who grew up in the area and was a fan of quintessential Swedish life and beauty. The landscape here is in many ways an archetype of the Swedish forest.

the maiden's pet dog and made themselves a home beside the rock. While Junker was away hunting, some of the father's men caught sight of the young woman and killed her dog with a spear, whereupon she wrestled the weapon from the attacker's grasp and poked his eye out, only for another of the men to attack her and hack her head off. When Junker returned to discover the macabre scene he fled, never to return. However, his ghost and the spirits of his relatives are said to have remained faithful to the rock and have scared and entranced many a forest-goer down the ages.

Tiveden lies between Lakes Vänern and Vättern, the two largest freshwater lakes in Sweden, and is a prime example of a joint valley landscape, a landform found in a wide band across the central part of the country. It is typified by the irregular, broken nature of the terrain and grey bedrock, once cracked and ruptured by earthquakes and faults. The plant life is more or less as one would expect, with barren pine forest on the higher ground and denser tracts of spruce in the valleys. No genuinely rare species occur, but Tiveden is world-famous for the red water lilies which grow at Lake Fagertärn and a few other lakes outside the park boundaries. The fauna is fairly typical for a mid-Swedish coniferous forest, though capercaillie and hazelhen both occur in good numbers, while the three-toed woodpecker can be found among stands of old-growth trees. Lynx also inhabit the park but are rarely seen.

In the Middle Ages Tiveden occupied a strategic position between the kingdoms of Götaland and Svealand and its forests were the scene of many a battle for royal power and influence. By the time King Gustav Vasa came to the throne in the sixteenth century, Tiveden was a notorious haunt of highwaymen and brigands. This notoriety has survived into the modern era, and Stigmanspasset (The Highwayman Pass) in the north of the park can still send a shiver down the spine. The narrow gravel track that runs through this joint valley is overlooked by high walls of rock that provide ideal cover for the ambushes that occurred periodically in bygone days. Highwaymen and robbers were not the only threat to travellers in those times; the presence of wolves also inspired fear and dread. Nowadays the forest is an altogether safer place, even if wolves – once hunted to extinction – have recently returned and roam freely once more.

Lake Trehörningen, the largest lake in the park, is a natural gem that in spring and summer echoes to the plaintive call of the black-throated diver. A colony of mew gulls breeds on the lake's rocky islets.

Stenkälla is a natural spring surrounded by huge boulders and is Tiveden's most famous spot. Novelist and poet Verner von Heidenstam, who won the Nobel Prize for Literature in 1916, grew up close by and immortalised the area in his poem "Tiveden".

An attractive sandy beach runs for several hundred metres along the northern shore of Lake Trehörningen. On dank autumn days, when the islets are shrouded in mist, the lake take on a special wild and lonely character. (Overleaf.)

GOTSKA SANDÖN

We have just disembarked on Gotska Sandön and are filled with a sense of being in the perfect location – in the middle of the Baltic Sea on a desert island with sandy beaches stretching for miles and not another human being in sight. It is never crowded here: strict regulations allow only a limited number of people on the island at any one time. The rules are there to protect Gotska Sandön's fragile ecosystem of sand dunes and pine forest. The nature in the island's interior is familiar and strange at the same time – and highly suggestive. The eye roves far between the pines that stand like columns in a huge, high-ceilinged room. Dense carpets of heather and reindeer moss creep low along the flat ground beneath them. Beyond the protection of the treetops, the sand is exposed and vulnerable to the elements.

We walk for miles in the tracks made by the offroad vehicles of the island's few permanent residents. Tramping through the loose, yielding sand is energy-sapping but allows us to reflect on the monotonous beauty of the pine forest. Little life is visible. The treetops murmur and sigh, reinforcing the loneliness and isolation of this remote Baltic outpost. Every now and then boughs creak as they touch in the gentle wind. The sea is hidden from view and barely audible, yet is ever-present amid the smell of salt carried on the breeze. Inside the woods, only the distant crash of waves on the beach interrupts the stillness. Groves of neatly interspersed pines a couple of kilometres long extend to the sea in all directions. Peace and quiet reigns inside these wooded arbours, a peaceful refuge on this windswept island of sand.

Most of all, Gotska Sandön is famous for its beaches. Long and expansive, they are Sweden's answer to the playas of the Mediterranean or South America. Names like Las Palmas, Franska Bukten (French Bay) and Pallas – all originating from local maritime history and events – underscore the exotic character of these sandy vistas.

Geologically, Gotska Sandön is the crest of a fifty-kilometre-long underwater reef of soft sand and moraine, from which it is seventy metres

Waves pound Stenrevet reef on Gotska Sandön's northern tip. Gale-force winds on days like this emphasise the island's exposed location and can cause serious beach erosion.

Large flocks of eider ducks congregate offshore during spring, when the cooing call of the drakes carries far on still days. Large numbers of long-tailed ducks also use the shallow coastal waters as a migration staging post.

The rough track between Fyr-byn Lighthouse and Tärnudden Point runs for almost ten kilometres though the pine forest that covers much of the island.

Large parts of Gotska Sandön's forest are primeval-like, with old-growth trees interspersed with the occasional hump-backed piece of fallen timber. Logging took place in the second half of the nineteenth century and a narrow-gauge railway was built in the 1920s.

The long, deserted beach of Las Palmas in the north of the island is thought to take its name from a ship wrecked nearby. Marram and lyme grass help to bind the sand and prevent erosion. (Overleaf.)

down to the Ordovician limestone bedrock. The sand and moraine dates back to the last Ice Age, when retreating glaciers left behind a moraine ridge that later became inundated with huge volumes of sand deposited by glacial meltwater. The sea level rose as the ice melted, but the land – no longer weighed down by ice – rose too, and the sands of Gotska Sandön gradually lifted from the sea, first emerging some five thousand years ago.

The island's highest point, Höga Åsen, is a fifty-metre-high sand dune. The shallow waters surrounding it contain two treacherous reefs, Salvorev and Kopparstenarna, which have claimed a host of wrecks down the ages. The reefs now form part of a large marine reserve that surrounds the national park and provides a vital habitat for marine life.

Though mostly flat, Gotska Sandön can be surprisingly rolling where the wind has blown the sand into piles and ridges. Myriad sand dunes, ranging from five to twenty metres high, criss-cross the island and act as a cordon protecting the beaches from erosion. Sometimes, though, the sea breaks through, and autumn storms can see chunks of land being gobbled up by the waves.

On the southern shore the beach is higher and narrower, and here the pine-clad coast rises twenty metres above the sea to provide a panoramic view of the Baltic. We arrive via the longest of the island's many sandy roads, which runs from the lighthouse in the north. Built in the mid-nineteenth century, the lighthouse brought a handful of full-time inhabitants to the island. Hunters and fishermen lived periodically on Gotska Sandön during prehistoric times, and the remains of large burial cairns indicate the early presence of seal hunters. Remnants of settlements from the early Middle Ages have also been found, and it is thought that Baltic pirates used the island as a land base.

The signing of the Treaty of Brömsebro in 1645 saw Gotska Sandön pass from Danish sovereignty into Swedish hands. One hundred and fifty years later, the Swedish state decided to parcel out land to tenant farmers, an initiative that heralded the arrival of more permanent dwellings. The new settlers cleared land at Gamla Gården in the south-west of the island, built enclosures and began farming crops and livestock. Various tenant farmers came and went before the arrival of Petter Gothberg, an infamous wrecker who lived on Gotska Sandön with his wife and two daughters from 1801 to 1828. A coarse, stocky man, Gothberg is said to have ridden along the shore on stormy nights on a lame horse, using the flickering

Bredsand is the widest beach and home to a large colony of lesser black-backed and herring gulls. By Swedish standards, the island has a paucity of large animals; grey seals, bats and hares are the only mammals which occur.

Northerly winds and high seas sometimes prevent the ferryboat from mooring at its favoured anchorage on the island's northern tip. Visitors disembark instead in landing dinghies at more sheltered spots, like here on the west coast.

The Schipka Pass is close to the highest point on the island. Its name comes from the scene of a battle in modern-day Bulgaria in 1877–78 and was coined in conjunction with a road-building project as an ironic response to constant newspaper reports of "No news from the Schipka Pass".

The pond at Kapellängen acts like a magnet for birds on an island where freshwater is in short supply. Here a chiffchaff pauses in a hazel tree before coming down to drink.

The shoreline turns pebbly at Varvsbukten on the southern tip of the island, where the pine-topped hill offers a spectacular view of the sunrise. (Overleaf.)

light from his lantern to trick seafarers into thinking they had reached safety. Legend has it that Gothberg lured stranded captains and crews to his barn at Gamla Gården, where after offering them food he shot them dead through cracks in the timber walls and then proceeded to plunder the beached vessels. It is known that Gothberg was convicted of wreck plundering, and a hut still stands on the site of the barn at Gamla Gården where he is said to have slain his victims.

A few decades later brought the arrival of another colourful character, a poor and destitute farmer's widow named Söderlund, whose desperate poverty prompted people on the nearby and much larger island of Gotland to collect money for her and her two sons and daughter. The funds were to provide her with decent clothes, and she became known ever after as Madam. She lived on the island for more than fifty years, and her son Hjalmar went on to become the lighthouse keeper.

TYRESTA

Just twenty kilometres from Stockholm city centre lies Tyresta National Park, one of the oldest and most unspoilt forests in southern Sweden. It is hard to believe that this forest wilderness is right on the doorstep of a city of more than one million people.

Tyresta hit the national headlines in 1999 when a major fire devastated large swathes of its pristine forest. Ten years on, the scars are still visible. Charred trunks and lifeless skeletons make the fire-ravaged area look like a mausoleum. Many of the damaged trees were toppled by a fierce storm the following autumn, leaving logs and brushwood in twisted piles on the forest floor. The blaze, which raged at ground level, took a severe toll on tree root systems in the four hundred and fifty hectare fire zone, weakening many trees that might otherwise have survived the flames.

Ironically, the fire launched Tyresta's international reputation. The destruction of such a large tract of protected and pristine forest was unprecedented in modern times, and biologists were soon queuing up to analyse the effects of the blaze.

The national park authority responded quickly to this surge of interest, building a path to allow access to the fire area. Over the last decade, scientists from far and wide have worked here, using the fire zone as an outdoor laboratory and discovering in the process a variety of animal and plant species new to science.

We pass a couple of makeshift gates made from sawn-off tree trunks and walk over the bare rocky surface, on which the habitual layer of lichen has yet to regrow. Green moss carpets the hollows and dense clusters of willow and birch grow in the damp fissures. Charred trees stand like sentinels everywhere, their sooty trunks contrasting with the green undergrowth and making the fire area look more like savannah than forest.

The wounded landscape is more dramatic than the coniferous forest that survived the flames and dominates the rest of the park. But although the unscathed areas may look ordinary, the appearance is beguiling.

The spring mating cry of a black-throated loon penetrates the mist over Lake Årsjön on an early summer's morning. According to local legend, a horse called the Ålsjö Whiteblaze inhabits the lake. The lake is poor in nutrients but has a suggestive hour-glass shape which divides it into three basins with two small channels between.

Female cuckoos do not call but wait for a suitable male to turn up. Cuckoos breed annually at Tyresta but have declined heavily across Sweden in recent decades. Those that breed in the national park often lay their eggs in the nest of the common redstart.

In fact they are unique. Few comparable areas of primeval forest exist in central Sweden. The national park stretches for mile after mile in all directions and is at the heart of a large forest landscape that extends well beyond its boundaries. Adjacent nature reserves provide protection for neighbouring forests, too. A patchwork of small lakes with alternately rocky and swampy beaches, interspersed with a few open mires, dots the landscape.

Tyresta's forest is ancient because it was spared from fire for several centuries – until the inferno of 1999. Indeed, it is the oldest area of woodland in the southern half of the country and the main reason why the area was chosen as a national park. The trees here have grown for hundreds of years free from the hazards of logging and fire, with the oldest specimens being around three hundred and fifty years old. This makes Tyresta a fascinating place for biologists.

But how did it manage to escape fires and the logger's axe? The main cause of forest fires down the ages (apart from lightning) was slash and burn clearance of woodland for agriculture. Farmers would light blazes to clear land, and sometimes these would rage out of control and destroy larger areas. Then came the rise of the iron industry, which was expanding so fast by the seventeenth century that the authorities banned slash and burn nationwide to guarantee sufficient supplies of firewood to make the charcoal needed to power the iron foundries. The new law was widely flouted, but not at Tyresta. Baron Gabriel Oxenstierna of nearby Tyresö made sure that the ban was strictly enforced, his sense of duty no doubt related to the fact that his brother, Chancellor Axel Oxenstierna, was the driving force behind it).

Rigid adherence to the prohibition on slash and burn, combined with rough terrain that made logging difficult, ensured that the forest remained unscathed by fire and axe. For several hundred years the trees were left to grow undisturbed – and unnoticed. Few people actually knew how special the forest was until a new landowner submitted plans to log the area in the 1930s. Word reached the head forester of Stockholm County about the logging initiative and he managed to persuade the city council to purchase the area to save it for posterity. Tyresta was preserved as a public recreation area and people began flocking from Stockholm to experience a taste of forest wilderness.

Scouts, orienteering enthusiasts, mushroom and berry pickers and hikers were among those attracted to this outdoor lung on the edge of the capital. A national inventory of Sweden's primeval forests in the 1980s resulted in Tyresta being upgraded first to a nature reserve and then to a national park. Looking back, Tyresta's journey is a shining example of Swedish conservation.

The national park is not just valuable biologically; it has a precious cultural heritage too. The village of Tyresta, just outside the park

Fanned by strong winds, the fire of August 1999 swept rapidly across the dry stony ground in the heart of the national park. Five hundred fire fighters with one hundred kilometres of hoses tackled the blaze. Twelve helicopters made five thousand flights dropping water and trying to douse the flames. A less intense fire occurred in the same area in 1914, before which the forest had been left unscorched for one hundred and thirty years. The oldest parts of the national park have not experienced fire for three hundred and fifty years, which is unique for southern Sweden.

The forest stands ghost-like in the aftermath of the fire – stripped of vegetation other than the moss that quickly regrew. This photograph was taken at Lake Stensjön, which is just visible between the trees.

Tyresta stands in a fissure valley that rises to a height of eighty metres and is criss-crossed by shallow valleys and hollows. Small bogs, like this patch of hair moss and sedge close to Lake Bylsjön, are found here and there.

boundary, dates back to the Iron Age, its picturesque meadows and pastures harking back to the rural Sweden of yesteryear. We take a walk in the forest north of the village, entering a landscape of rocky outcrops and numerous oddly shaped trees. Pine trees line one of the crags as if on parade: gnarled and smooth, twisted and straight, thick and skinny, young and old. Dry stumps and fallen logs bear witness to the natural cycle of life and death.

Though far from flat, the forest offers few good lookout points, making it hard to judge its size and scale, though here and there one can catch a glimpse of high-rise apartment blocks in Stockholm's southern suburbs. So close and yet a world away.

With their smooth, glistening surfaces, Tyresta's scenic lakes stand as islands of light in the dark forest. Flanked by barren coniferous forest and a stony shoreline, Lake Årsjön, in particular, exudes a sense of the wild and untamed.

Tyresta's sounds are also unique. On calm days one can hear the silence that is unique to old forests, but more often it is the distant hum

of road traffic on the busy motorways running to and from Stockholm that carries on the wind. From the edge of the park one hears the city itself: car engines accelerating, doors closing, people calling, the tinny jingle of an ice-cream van piercing through the springtime birdsong. As these artificial sounds of modern society reverberate among the centuries-old trees we understand the true essence of Tyresta National Park – and what a special place it is.

The size of Tyresta's forest is evident from the air, with Lake Årsjön on the left and Lake Bylsjön on the right. The area hit by fire in 1999 stands out as a brownish patch amid the sea of green. In the distance is the Stockholm suburb of Tyresö.

A small road built for fire engines passes the tallest stands of trees in the forest en route to Lake Bylsjön.

The wailing call of black-throated loons echoes across some of Tyresta's nine lakes during late spring and early summer. Loon comes from the Icelandic word "lómr", meaning cry or wail.

Deadwood is symbolic of old coniferous forest and is plentiful at Tyresta. Dead pines like this one can remain standing for many years thanks to the resin in their trunks.

Fog over Lake Stensjön on a chilly October morning. This rocky outcrop rises thirty metres above the water and was once the site of an ancient castle used for defensive purposes in times of unrest. It is thought that people used the castle during the Great Migration fifteen hundred years ago.

The rocky outcrop rises steeply from Lake Stensjön, which at eighteen metres is the deepest in the national park. Geologically this rock formation looks as if it might have been caused by a fault, but it is probably due to deep weathering in the granite bedrock. (Overleaf.)

ÄNGSÖ

If any Swedish national park deserves comparison with the Garden of Eden, it is the island of Ängsö. The question is whether early summer or autumn is closest to paradise: when blooming cowslips and other wildflowers deck the ground in irresistible beauty, or when the burnished October leaves bathe the woods in seasonal splendour? In truth, Ängsö is at its finest at both times. The countryside in this part of the Roslagen archipelago, north of Stockholm, is never less than gorgeous. Picturesque small roads and carefully tended stone walls are part of the charm, relics of a bygone rural landscape. A corridor of fields and meadows bisects the island, forging a sudden and sharp contrast between the pastoral and the wild. Dark spruce forest covers much of Ängsö (to the surprise of many visitors expecting a more agricultural landscape). Most of the trees have stood untouched for generations, though some selected felling takes place nowadays on the western half of the island to recreate the former farmed woodland environment.

Only the cultivated parts of Ängsö, the haymaking meadows especially, were considered important when the national park was established in 1909. One hundred years on, the meadows are in robust health and we spot a group of roe deer grazing at the edge of the forest as we pass Stormaren, in the centre of the island. A ferry bound for Finland, its hull towering like a skyscraper, passes serenely behind the trees. The wet meadow at Stormaren was once a narrow channel separating two islands, but the process of post-glacial rebound gradually lifted the channel until it became dry, and the two islands merged in the late eighteenth century.

Since then, man has set the tone on Ängsö. A crofter settled at Stormaren in 1725 and began converting the overgrown channel into a hay meadow and felling trees for timber and firewood. Within seventy or so years the island was virtually treeless. By the time Ängsö was declared a national park a hundred years or so later, the crofter's cottage had been leased out. The occupant was given permission to stay – but only on condition that he refrained from cutting the meadows. At the time, the Royal Swedish

Cowslips abound in spring across the island, including here at Stenbacken, and elder-flowered orchids add to the splendour. The early marsh-orchid, the lesser butterfly-orchid and the rare bird's eye primrose also grow here.

Ängsö's birdlife is rich and varied. Great-crested grebes nest at Hemviken and during spring pairs engage in a spectacular water dance. White-tailed eagles breed in the coniferous forest on the east of the island.

Clover and buttercups grow in the meadows of Stormaren, once a narrow sea channel that cut the island in two. One sixth of Ängsö is covered by meadows.

The picturesque hazelwoods at Stormaren turn golden and russet in autumn. Picking hazelnuts is not allowed under Sweden's right to roam legislation due to an old medieval law that forbade the pillaging of hazelwoods.

Academy of Sciences took the view that leaving the meadows uncut and ungrazed would benefit the local flora – a glaring error eventually highlighted by botanist Lars-Gunnar Romell in the 1930s. By then, many of Ängsö's meadows were overgrown and in disuse. A proposed restoration project foundered due to uncertainty over who would carry out the work and how it would be funded, though a house was built for an island superintendent. However, it was not until conservation issues began to gain ground in the 1960s that regular work began to preserve Ängsö's cultural landscape.

Now well managed, the national park is a wildlife and cultural gem. It is the perfect destination for anyone wanting to gain a taste of what archipelago life was like in bygone days, and the natural harbours at Svartviken and Norrviken throng with boats during the spring and summer.

Oaks are the oldest trees on the island, some of them around five hundred years old. Stone walls surround the pastures and wild chervil and buttercups grow in the meadows.

Hemudden is the site of Ängsö's old farm and now home to the island superintendent. Cattle graze in the meadows, tree pollarding is done in the traditional manner and a few fields of crops are grown too.

The striae in the rock east of Hemviken were caused by shifting glaciers. The island consists of gneiss and granite bedrock covered primarily with moraine and clay soil. The old farm has been here since the start of the 1800s, though new buildings have been added since. (Overleaf.)

GARPHYTTAN

Garphyttan's meadows awaken feelings of tenderness and nostalgia. Generations toiled hard for centuries to transform the once dense forest into an idyllic pasture for horses and cattle. The intricate interplay between farmer, land and animals encouraged wild flowers to bloom and softened the countryside. If forests are the archetypal Swedish landscape, then meadows are their smile – and it is this gentle scenery that Garphyttan epitomises. In spring, large numbers of people come with picnic baskets to experience the national park's rural charm and the impressive carpets of spring flowers growing among the groves of deciduous trees.

The area looks the way it does today due to the efforts of the yeomen of Kilsbergen – three farmers who lived here for many years until the early nineteenth century. Of their settlement at Östra Gården Svenshyttan, only the house foundations remain today, but their legacy lives on the surrounding meadows and pastures. A map of the area from 1822 shows the existence of small irregular patchworks of fields, suggesting that the land was farmed long before the map was drawn. The land changed again later on, when some of the meadows were ploughed for crop growing. The Garphytte Bruk ironworks gradually bought the three farms and in 1870 felled all the forest in the area. The iron industry was in its heyday and the wood was used to make charcoal to power the foundries.

At about this time a German forester moved into the area and replanted the forest – with spruce trees from his native country. These imported trees are now more than one hundred years old and have not been thinned since the national park was founded in 1909. The only naturally occurring vegetation within the park boundaries is an old pinewood on Svensbodaberget Hill.

The beautiful meadows at Garphyttan are admired by many people, yet the national park also raises a question or two. The rules state that all national parks should be large areas with natural and, ideally, virgin landscape. But like Dalby Söderskog in southernmost Sweden, Garphyttan is small and heavily influenced by human activity. That it is a national

Thousands of wood anemones bloom in spring at Rånnlyckan, with smaller numbers of hepatica in the background. The national park is covered by moraine, which provides nutrient-rich soil in the meadows. A large number of meadows were converted to fields in the nineteenth century, but many have since been restored and are cut every year to preserve them.

Old apple trees also grow on Garphyttan's meadows.

The trimmed ash trees at Sten-lyckan stand proud like temple pillars. Ash was once favoured for pollarding because it produces lots of shoots, which in past eras were used as animal fodder.

The escarpment that separates the three hundred-metre-high Kilsbergen Hills from the Närke plain in the east is visible from Svensbodaberget Hill. This part of the national park is more dramatic than the pastoral meadows lower down. The Bergslagsleden hiking trail passes through here.

Budding sycamore trees in spring at Stenlyckan meadow, where wood anemones are already in bloom (overleaf).

park at all is really an accident of history. It followed the government's purchase of Östra Gården Svenshyttan farm as part of Sweden's first nature conservation programme. A state forestry company then suggested that the meadows closest to the farm be designated a national park. A bit of a wrangle then ensued, with the county council lobbying for the park to cover a larger area. But in the end a zoology professor from the Royal Swedish Academy of Sciences decided that only the farm and adjacent land would be included. Paradoxically, this saw the German spruces planted a few decades earlier being incorporated within the park boundaries. This is out of keeping with modern principles and has prompted some people to call for Garphyttan to be downgraded to a nature reserve. But local people are fiercely proud of the park and determined to keep it. A pragmatic solution would be to treat the small national parks together and regard them simply as monuments to a bygone era. That way, they could be allowed to continue as exceptions to the rule rather than standard-bearers of modern national park policy.

FÄRNEBOFJÄRDEN

The Dalälven River has long been seen as marking the boundary between northern and southern Sweden. In biogeographical terms the river and its environs are known as "Limes Norrlandicus" – a zone in which northern and southern plant and animal species meet and coexist side by side. Here, southern deciduous tree species such as oak rub shoulders with the taiga forest that holds sway farther north and beyond. Fjärnebofjärden National Park, one of Sweden's finest, graces this area of rich biodiversity and offers a wealth of fascinating encounters with physical geography. Through it flows the Dalälven River, the third longest in the country and whose network of wide fjords confers a unique character and quality on the park's vast forests.

These majestic, shifting waters are Färnebofjärden's lifeblood and pulse. The river rises from its source high in the hills of Dalarna four hundred kilometres away, entering the national park via the rapids of Tyttboforsen and then flowing through Fjärnebofjärden's network of fjords and inlets (forty percent of the park is water) before exiting via the another set of rapids at Gysingeforsarna. Thereafter the river proceeds through similar country on its final one-hundred-kilometre stretch to the Gulf of Bothnia in the Baltic Sea. The River Dalälven once took a different course and flowed into Lake Mälaren, but glacial meltwater at the end of the Ice Age left a high esker that took it in a new direction over the flatlands of North Uppland.

It is through these flatlands that the river flows today. The low-lying terrain lacks good vantage points but a multitude of islets and islands make for a varied landscape. Major seasonal fluctuations in the river level have a strong effect on the national park's plant and animal life. In spring the riverside meadows flood, creating mangrove-like thickets of flooded roots. Some species, such as the aspen, thrive due to these natural ebbs and flows. The park is a varied mosaic of dense forest, open mires, rushing riverbeds, narrow tributaries, wide expanses of open water, flood-meadows and hundreds of scattered islets. This diversity makes Fjärnebofjärden a

An old oak by the Tyttbo-forsen rapids. This tree species prospers in the riverine sediment and mild waterside climate. Seasonal floods mean that Stoltorpet cabin on the other side of the River Dalälven is one of very few buildings in the national park, though a number of old hay-making barns, now mostly derelict, remain standing.

Black grouse perform court-ship displays on the bogs south of Tinäset in spring-time. A rich variety of breed-ing and migrant bird species makes the area a magnet for birdwatchers.

At Gysinge the river divides into two branches, which then themselves subdivide into smaller waterways. All form part of the River Dalälven's intricate system. The photograph shows a watercourse east of Mattön island during the spring flood.

Fishermen hoping for a bite at Skekarsbosjön, one of Färnebofjärden's many large bays. Grayling, pike, pike-perch and perch all occur naturally in the river.

With its large expanses of water and numerous sand and bedrock islands, Färnebofjärden can feel more like a lake than a river. (Overleaf.)

paradise for hikers, birdwatchers, botanists, mushroom pickers, anglers, canoeists and winter skiers and skaters. Access is easiest by water, a canoe allowing easy exploration of the various river tributaries. One autumn day finds us canoeing from the Dalälven fjords into Tiån, a small stream that feeds the river and leads into the heart of the national park. The summertime admittance restrictions, in place to avoid disturbance to breeding birds, have been lifted and we coast quietly along the narrow stream, fringed on either side by yellowing reedbeds. Behind the reeds lies a mire and beyond it the dark forest looms above the low countryside. The isolation is palpable: the nearest town is miles away and there are no man-made sounds to disturb the silence. Lake Tisjön is flat as a millpond in the crisp autumnal air.

On reaching Tinäset, Färnebofjärden's best-known area, one is immediately struck by a feeling of untamed wilderness (though the park as a whole is certainly not untouched as considerable areas of forest were logged during the latter part of the last century). Other areas have long stood free from human interference, however, and the oldest trees are found on the larger islands like Torrön and Vedön.

The Gysinge rapids are often open in December, when the air is dank from mist and fog. Dippers and long-tailed tits can be seen flying along the river. (Previous page.)

The River Storån as it enters Östaviken Bay. The critically endangered white-backed woodpecker can still be found in the area shown on the left side of the photograph.

A tributary of the River Storån leads to Lindebergsmossen Bog.

The viewing platform at Skekarsbo provides a prime vantage point over Färnebofjärden National Park (overleaf).

A crescent of dense coniferous forest stretches from Tinäset to the River Storån, one of the River Dalälven's largest tributaries in these parts. Pioneering surveys of this area by a group of ornithologists in the late 1960s found all Sweden's woodpecker species breeding here, alongside other bird species usually confined to undisturbed wildernesses. This news coincided with growing pressure for increased logging, triggering a battle between conservationists and landowners over Fjärnebofjärden's future. Fortunately from a nature conservancy standpoint, the authorities agreed to establish several reserves to protect the most valuable habitats – and in 1989 the area was included in the government's national parks plan. A decade later, Färnebofjärden formally opened as a national park.

HAMRA

When founded in 1909, Hamra was a minnow in national park terms — no bigger than twenty-seven football pitches in size. A major upgrade in 2011 extended the park boundaries more than fiftyfold, creating a protected zone that meets contemporary requirements for national park dimensions. We follow the trail through ancient coniferous forest in the main core of the park — a veritable oasis in a region known for its intensive logging tradition. The park, located in Orsa Finnmark, a remote part of Dalarna in west-central Sweden, has benefited greatly from enlargement. Today it combines coniferous forest of varying age with extensive marshlands nestling beneath rocky ridges and crags. One of the marshes, Svartåmyran, is a large and complex wetland dotted with islets and served by the River Svartån, which passes through a magnificent ravine. The river has miraculously escaped the fate of many others that have been dammed for hydropower or dredged for log driving.

Hamra found itself on the list of the country's first national parks in 1909 due to growing interest at the time in unspoilt countryside, with the Royal Swedish Academy of Sciences' nature conservation committee of the day describing Hamra as "the strangest area of primeval woodland that probably exists among all Sweden's forests". The committee envisaged the park as a place of scientific study, though some forestry experts countered that the protected area was too small to allow scientists to draw representative conclusions from their research. The argument was eventually settled after the academy's Einar Lönnberg visited the area and recommended that national park status be granted.

At the time, Hamra was owned by the state and encompassed twenty-eight thousand hectares of untouched forest. Untouched, that is, apart from a little farming by immigrant Finns and limited felling for firewood and timber, though in more recent times scientists have found pollen grains in the park's bogs whose presence indicate that the Finnish settlers burnt the woodland to create open pastures for their livestock and for crop farming.

The original parts of the national park provide an instructive example of

Lungwort growing on a sallow in the western part of Hamra National Park. Nowadays this lichen species is found only in very old forests. It is sensitive to air pollution and has declined heavily in Sweden, though still thrives at Hamra.

Sundew – a plant species that captures small insects with its mucilaginous glands and uses moisture to digest them – grows on the bog behind Näckrostjärnen Lake and is widespread across the rest of Sweden. Few flowering plant species occur at Hamra.

Näckrostjärnen Lake at dusk. This small area of water is surrounded by open bogland in almost all directions. From here we look east.

An old fallen pine is reflected in the tiny pool on the national park's southern perimeter. Two surveys carried out seventy years apart have revealed that the pine population at Hamra is declining, while spruce is on the increase.

how primeval forest develops through natural renewal on land spared from the logger's axe. The age of the woods is palpable when walking through the park: giant pines three to four hundred years old with trunks up to eighty centimetres wide at chest height, and a dense brushwood of dead and decaying trees. The numerous boulders accentuate the ruggedness of the terrain. Scars on the deadwood and some of the pines testify to forest fires in bygone days. At least five blazes have swept Hamra since the eighteenth century. Thanks to their bark, pines can often withstand fires, and the species grows back well on scorched ground. In damper areas, spruce predominates. The land in the park is mostly dry, but at Näckrostjärnen, a small lake that forms an almost perfect circle, there is an open quagmire. Svansjön Lake and a much smaller unnamed pool mark the northern and southern boundaries, but these are the only watercourses in the park.

The relatively large Lake Svansjön lies at an elevation of more than four hundred metres above sea level. The extension of the national park in 2011 brought both the lake and the marshlands to the north within the park borders.

Siberian jays are fearless and found in old coniferous forests like those at Hamra, though the species has declined generally in Sweden. The park's otherwise unremarkable wildlife is notable for an extraordinary profusion of beetles, which flourish thanks to all the dead wood. Four hundred and fifty species have been recorded.

FULUFJÄLLET

The Fulufjället mountain range in the province of Dalarna is a geological one-off. When experts began trying to establish the age of its many boulder fields, they were amazed at what they found. During the Ice Age, the inland glaciers remained virtually stationary at Fulufjället. This was because the base of the ice became frozen solid to the ground, which prevented the usual grinding action caused by glacial movements. Thus Fulufjället remained intact more or less in its ancient state, unlike virtually everywhere else in Sweden, where the shifting ice typically scoured the terrain like a scraper. This unusual geological phenomenon meant that melting glacial water instead played the major hand in shaping the lie of the land during the Ice Age. Rivers of melting ice gouged out numerous gullies on Fulufjället's slopes. More densely vegetated than the surrounding fell plateaus, these run in long parallel lines and, from a distance, make the mountainsides look like lines on a page.

The Ice Age is not the only reason why Fulufjället is unusual. Geologically, the area does not belong to the Scandinavian Caledonian chain. The bedrock here is not granite or gneiss, as mostly found in Sweden, but sandstone – which can be used to make sharpening stones. The sandstone here is more than a billion years old and was formed by grains of sand falling to the bottom of an Equatorial sea. For hundreds of millions of years, the continental drift and mountain building caused by shifts in the Earth's tectonic plates gradually nudged the sandstone slowly northwards as volcanic magma pushed it to the surface. Eventually it ended up at Fulufjället.

At Fulufjället National Park one can see this ancient, often rose-tinted sandstone in all its glory from the canyon at Njupeskär. This deep ravine is fed by the cascading waters of Sweden's largest waterfall and is the jewel in the park's crown. At the head of the canyon the tumbling water eats ever further into the rock behind, a nice illustration of retrogressive erosion. The magnificent waterfall attracts thousands of visitors every year and is reached via a popular wooden trail that runs over the rocky ground.

Göljådalen Valley starts with a deep canyon that cuts into Fulufjället's east face. Göljåstöten, the peak in the background, is 915 metres above sea level. The thick carpet of reindeer moss signals the absence of reindeer, for which the moss is a favourite food. Violent rains in August 1997 caused flash flooding in the hills to turn the stream on the canyon floor into a raging torrent.

A dipper feeds its young by a stream. This bird species, found across Sweden, is common in the national park's waterways. It curtsies daintily on stones and rocks while scanning the water for small invertebrates.

At a height of ninety-three metres and a free fall of seventy metres, Njupeskär is Sweden's highest waterfall. The exact height was something of a bone of contention in the past, with conflicting nineteenth century sources suggesting the true figure was one hundred and twenty five metres or one hundred and forty metres.

In winter Njupeskär is like a huge church organ, with pipes of blue and reddish ice. The frozen water is popular with ice climbers at this time of year.

These boulder fields high on the Fulufjället plateau are among the oldest geological landforms found in Sweden. The sandstone rocks pre-date the Ice Age. Some have ribs like washboards, and these petrified ripple marks date back to when the rock lay as sand on the seabed, one billion or so years ago. (Overleaf.)

High, though not especially voluminous, the falls are observed from a wooden viewing platform.

Fulufjället forms a large plateau not unlike the table mountains found in deserts, and this topography is very different from typical Swedish mountain scenery. Following the trail from the canyon and up to the top, we are greeted by an endless rolling plain of bushy heath and ancient boulder fields. Such an open vista is a liberating sight. In the far distance, the strangely shaped summit of Mount Städjan rises above the skyline. The high rocky slopes that descend from the plateau in all directions make Fulufjället look like a table or platform – a barren island surrounded by forest. The park boundary follows the national border with Norway, which lies to the west and is readily visible from the plateau.

Beneath our feet lies a layer of sandstone twelve hundred metres thick. Molten lava once poured through cracks in the rock and in some places the black diabase formed where the hot lava congealed can be seen today. Over time, diabase crumbles into angular columns, one of which has turned Skarvhammaren into a challenging sixty-metre rock face that plunges into the forest below. The sides of the Njupeskär canyon are also vertical but are of sandstone and even higher, around one hundred metres. But Fulufjället is more than sheer rock faces. In the south and north of the park the slopes are gentler. Sandstone is often stratified, resulting in horizontal cracks when the rock loosens and crumbles. Many of the flatter areas, for instance the dry river beds, resemble quarries.

On the upland heaths it as if we have arrived in a new world. When the renowned Swedish naturalist Carl Linnaeus visited Dalarna in 1734 he only caught a glimpse of Fulufjället. "In the west, when passing on the road, the great Fulufjällen was seen ten kilometres away…" he wrote in his diary. The plateau, which ranges from nine hundred to more than one thousand metres above sea level, is a vestige of the ancient and expansive plains once formed by land erosion. Long before the Ice Age, the movement of the Earth's crust created fault-lines, after which came erosion. Fulufjället was initially pushed up high and has since been whittled down by the elements to its current height. Although the mountain range differs geologically from other Swedish fells, the plateau looks more or less the same as a typical fell below the tree line. And indeed, a genuine geological tie does exist because when the Scandinavian fells emerged from the sea around four hundred million years ago they eventually merged with Fulufjället, since when the area has followed the same geological pattern as the rest of the Scandinavian fells.

The vegetation at Fulufjället is unique. A combination of nutrient-poor bedrock and a continental climate mean heather and reindeer moss grow here, the latter forming impressively dense carpets that cushion the feet as one walks. The abundance of reindeer moss has a simple explanation: Sami reindeer herders have never used the area to graze their animals.

The sparse woodland at Brottbäckstjärn below Mount Fulufjället is eight hundred metres above sea level. The forests of northern Dalarna stretch from Nipfjället to the left and Städjan to the right. The coniferous forest that encircles the Fulufjället plateau has experienced fires and logging down the years but still contains pristine parts with old-growth trees. Pine dominates, while spruce grows in damper areas. Mountain birch grows only in a narrow belt below the tree line, apart from in the north of the park, where it is more widespread. Brown bears and lynx both inhabit the park.

All hell broke loose on August 30, 1997, when four hundred millimetres of rain fell on Fulufjället in the worst storm to hit the area since the Ice Age. Enormous volumes of water cascaded into the gullies and the River Göljån swelled to more than five hundred times its normal size. The torrent swept away huge quantities of earth and reduced the forest to sticks. The River Göljån's lower reaches are now a tourist attraction and a reminder of nature's power.

The Njupeskär waterfall cascades into a deep canyon gouged out by the falling water over a long period of time. Precipitous rock faces tower above the walking trail and the observation platform in front of the falls. A burial mound from 400–500 A.D. can be found nearby, indicating that paths have long existed on Fulufjället. (Overleaf.)

The red sandstone ledges in Fulufjället's canyons are an ideal nesting site for gyr-falcons, an endangered bird of prey that breeds here irregularly. Only a hundred or so pairs of the species breed in Sweden, all confined to the country's fells and uplands. The gyrfalcon's staple food is grouse and breeding com-mences as early as late February. Falcon trapping is thought to have occurred here in the past. Linnaeus noted in his diary that falcons were captured in northern Dalarna and sent to aristocrats and nobles all over the world. The remains of a stone circle at Tangsjöstugan are thought to be a former trapper's hut. Either that or they were an altar for outdoor religious ceremonies along the pilgrim route that crosses the moun-tain. No-one knows for sure.

Wild reindeer did occur in earlier times, according to Linnaeus, but the land has been spared from grazing for many centuries now. The grassy plains, with the occasional juniper bush dotted here and there, are easily explored on foot once one has climbed the rock face up onto the plateau. There is a well-developed system of trails and log cabins where hikers and other visitors can camp for the night. Some of the trails pass the large network of lakes in the northern part of the park. These waters have been treated with lime to combat acidification, ensuring their preservation as top-quality fishing locations for the adventurous angler. Salmon trout and char are top of the menu.

Man's presence at Fulufjället dates back many centuries, and a pilgrim route is thought to have passed over the plateau in former times. One trail, Jämtvägen, was used in winter when the area belonged to Norway in the late Middle Ages. Numerous other paths and trails existed in the days when farmers would move out into the hills with their animals for summer grazing. Some of the old summer farm cottages are still in use today, while others are derelict.

Fulufjället became a new type of national park when it was established in 2002. After encountering initial local opposition to the park plans, the authorities worked hard to gain the support and confidence of local people. They had learned the lessons of past mistakes in the Swedish fells, where other proposed parks were fiercely opposed by local people, who saw them as a threat to their freedom. Furufjället tackled this issue by establishing four zones with different levels of protection, enabling rules and regulations to be adapted to people's interests without compromising the purpose of the national park. The authorities have also made a major effort to harness public interest in the park by developing tourism and building a visitor's and exhibition centre near the village of Mörkret.

TÖFSINGDALEN

Visit Töfsingdalen if you really want to know what inaccessible means. This national park, concealed deep in the remote and roadless tracts of northern Dalarna province, is physically challenging in all respects. A couple of hiking trails lead to the national park boundary but the area itself is pathless and extremely demanding for the walker. The huge rocks and boulders that litter the terrain make walking here a bone-crunching experience. The trees are sparsely spaced among the rocks, and the boulders "wantonly scattered over disconsolately wide areas," in the words of Professor Karl-Herman Forsslund in 1926. Deep holes and clefts bar the way at every turn.

These rock-strewn tracts lie in a valley between the Olåsen and Hovden ridges, whose stony sides protrude from a mountain range further to the north. The name Olåsen means boulder field and describes the lie of the land. Seen from afar, the slopes look like a patchwork of scattered trees growing between gaps and crevices in the rocky ground. The reason why there are so many boulders dates back to the end of the Ice Age, when the retreating glaciers scooped up rocks from the surface and carried them a brief distance before dumping them in piles on the slopes.

Exploring the park, one might imagine that the unusual proliferation of rocks and boulders was why Töfsingdalen became a national park. In fact, the park was given protection for one simple reason: to protect a breeding pair of golden eagles on Hovden's west-facing slope. This was in 1925 and followed a campaign by people in the nearby village of Idre and a crown forest keeper by the name of Edvard Bergström. The site was the southernmost breeding location for golden eagles known in Sweden at that time. The following year, the Swedish Society of Nature Conservation asked Professor Forsslund to conduct a biological survey of the area. He was deeply impressed by the untouched wilderness-like scenery, especially the luxuriant forest along the River Töfsingån, and recommended that the entire valley be given formal protection as a national park – a wish later granted by the government.

Mighty pines, some dead or dying, on the western slope of Hovden, with Mount Storvätteshågna – the highest peak in Dalarna province at one thousand one hundred and eighty-three metres – in the background. Though limited logging occurred in the area in the late nineteenth century, Töfsingdalen remains a pristine wilderness.

Wolf lichen, a species that has declined in the last century, grows on many of the dry pine trunks. Its poisonous sap causes asphyxia and was once used to poison wolves.

The River Storån alternates between rushing rapids and calmer, lagoon-like stretches. It marks the national park boundary.

Though gentle in parts, the River Töfsingån has a number of rocky waterfalls.

The slopes of Mount Stor-vätteshågna provide a picture-postcard view of the valley towards the bare top of Hovden, at almost nine hundred metres above sea level. Tofsingdalen's rocky terrain shows well between the trees. (Overleaf.)

We pick our way through the boulders to the verdant riverside spruce forest. The ground is damper here, with small pools and patches of marshland. But even among the trees there are rocks and slabs strewn everywhere. The forest includes many old tree specimens, and beneath them a lush carpet of lady and ostrich ferns covers the ground. It is a little like walking in a tropical rainforest. Baneberry and lily of the valley, which depend on nutrient-rich soil, grow here alongside a wealth of other plant species. Spruce is relatively uncommon in this part of Sweden; pine tends to dominate due to a continental climate and a soil poor in nutrients. Mountain birch also has a limited range in these southern climes but does occur in stunted bush-like stretches on the upper slopes of the Olåsen ridge.

The waters of the River Töfsingån eventually flow into the River Dalälven, Sweden's third largest river, after first feeding the River Storån, which forms the national park's southern boundary. Here, beavers have felled numerous riverside trees, in some places creating peaceful pools that intersperse the stretches of fast-flowing water.

SONFJÄLLET

Mount Sonfjället is one of the most famous landmarks in Sweden's southern mountains. This national park in the middle of sparsely populated Härjedalen province spans an entire mountain range and adjacent forests. But the main peak, Mount Sonfjället, stands alone, an impregnable stronghold with its steep rocky sides. The spectacular alpine summit is beguilingly beautiful, especially when seen from the east. An unbroken carpet of coniferous forest leads up to the mountain, confirming the national park in my eyes as a classic North Scandinavian landscape. Extensive, forest-clad ridges punctuated by isolated bare mountains are archetypal of this part of Sweden.

Unusually for a Swedish national park, one can drive round the park perimeter. Inside the park boundaries lies an untamed wilderness that contrasts starkly with the intensively managed forests which encircle it. When planning to create the country's first national parks in 1909, the authorities wanted to find an area of Sweden's southern mountains not used for reindeer herding. The choice fell on Sonfjället because the government owned forest land nearby. The absence of reindeer meant that a profuse layer of lichen and moss carpeted the mountain plateau, and this remains true today. Sonfjället differs dramatically from other mountain regions in this respect, and the light-grey reindeer moss that grows here is lush and dense. Nevertheless, pressure for grazing pasture has increased in recent decades and reindeer find their way into the park more and more often, their impact visible directly in the state of the ground vegetation.

A century ago Sonfjället was one of the last refuges in Sweden of the brown bear, which was in heavy decline due to hunting. When numbers of this mighty mammal began to recover in the second half of the century, Sonfjället was one of the main population centres from which the animals spread. Sweden has a healthy brown bear population nowadays, and chances of catching a glimpse of a bear – from a distance at least – are pretty good inside the national park, though bears are by nature shy creatures that tend to spend most of their time in the forests, making them

Mount Sonfjället rises eight hundred metres over Hedeviken Bay. Local people in Härjedalen province spell it Sonfjället, but this usage has not been followed since 1915 and is seen as archaic. Sonfjället is the spelling used on maps and in other official contexts. According to linguists, the name may derive from Sonnefjäll, meaning "sun" in Icelandic.

A dozen or so different brown bears inhabit the Sonfjället area, where each animal has its own favoured haunts. Bears were threatened by extinction in Sweden a century ago and the national park was their last refuge when it was founded. The species has since recovered and the Swedish population stands at around two thousand seven hundred.

A large cairn stands on the summit of Mount Sonfjället, one thousand two hundred and seventy-seven metres above sea level. The panoramic view covers the entire province of Härjedalen, including Mount Helags and Lunndörren Valley. Hills and peaks stretch wave-like in all directions, and the seven-hundred-metre-high Mount Søln is just visible one hundred kilometres to the west across the Norwegian border.

Alpine lady-fern grows in the deep ravine through which the Hällbäcken stream flows on Mount Sonfjället's northern slope. The ravines are also rich in moss.

harder to see. Lynx also occur regularly within the park as do wolverines, the latter more sporadically. The occasional wolf also passes through, meaning that all Sweden's four large predators occur at Sonfjället.

One might think that the presence of large carnivores would deter cattle farmers from keeping herds in the area, but old-fashioned livestock rearing still continues at Sonfjället. A small summer farm at Nyvallen, in a nature reserve adjacent to the national park and directly below Mount Sonfjället's steepest face, is still used by cattle owners who bring their livestock here in summer to graze in the forest. This old tradition of allowing domestic animals to wander freely in the forest is known as transhumance and involves the herders living temporarily in the wilds during the grazing season. As yet, no livestock losses have been recorded, though the herders accept it is a constant risk. Transhumance is an ancient tradition in Scandinavia and was practised widely in Sweden, throughout most of Norway and also in parts of Finland. Nonetheless, the presence of cattle munching peacefully on undergrowth in the mountain birch forest makes a slightly peculiar sight for the hiker exploring these remote uplands.

Mount Sonfjället reflected in the lake by the village of Hedeviken. The small livestock herders' cabin at Nyvallen is directly below the highest rock face. (Previous page.)

The birch forest on Mount Korpflyet's western slope bathed in evening sunlight as the coniferous forest behind falls into shadow.

Hästtjärn Mere gleams like a beady eye in the dawn sunlight. This tiny body of water between Mount Korpflyet and Mount Högfjället was once used for horse pasture during summer.

The mountain birch, or downy birch to give the proper name, grows in a belt of varying size round the mountain range. The ground around Nyvallen and to the north and east is damp, and here the forest is denser and taller, while the birches are more bush-like and sparsely scattered on the drier ground in the south and west of the national park. Sonfjället's southerly location and continental climate means that the few scattered birches on the slope of Mount Korpflyet, the southernmost peak in the park, grow at an altitude of eleven hundred metres. Only in one other place in Sweden does the tree-line go higher. Climate change is likely to shift the tree-line further up the mountainside in future.

Lower down, pine dominates the coniferous forest. Here and there the trees grow in impressive column-like stands, and one such is found along the trail beside the River Valmen, which forms the national park's eastern boundary. Here, the pines thrive in the sandy soil once scattered here by glacial deposits. Primeval-type forest covers more than half of the national park. Parts of the forest were logged a hundred years ago and some of the oldest trees were lost, but time is healing the scars and Sonfjället's forests are grand and imposing to the modern eye. Spruce is confined mainly to

the hillier ground and the numerous gullies and ravines. Here the forest is largely untouched, and some of the trees are up to two hundred and fifty years old.

Another transhumance shelter is found on the western side of Mount Sonfjället at Nysätern in another of the nature reserves that adjoin the national park. It serves snacks and refreshments and is a popular starting point for hikers intent on exploring the park's innermost areas. One can hike to Sododalen Valley and stay overnight in a sleeping cabin overlooked by a ring of the park's tallest peaks. Downy birch and plants like angelica and alpine blue-sow-thistle form a rich carpet of plant life along the stream that flows through the valley. The mountains themselves are of quartzite, an acidic rock that gives poor soil quality and creates grey vermiculations in the landscape. When ice and frost break open the rocks, the snow-white quartzite emerges to provide a dash of brightness.

With its slopes that once gushed with great floods of glacial meltwater, the Sonfjället massif is a living example of physical geography. Between Gråsidan and Mount Valmfjället the water gouged out a deep pass through

Dawn at Valmenvägen, a narrow gravel road east of the mountain range. Most of the forest around the road has been logged up to the River Valmen, which forms the national park boundary.

Swedish mountain cattle and Swedish red poll cattle graze in the forest below Mount Lillfjället. The hornless Swedish mountain cow was first bred in the mid-1880s for its high milk production. It is white with small red and black spots.

The morning sun illuminates the gush channels on Mount Gråsidan. These channels were once sculpted by glacial meltwater. Sonfjället's natural history and geology make it a fascinating place for scientists.

This solitary pine tree grows at an altitude of eight hundred metres on Mount Korpflyet – unusually high for this species. Climate change is likely to see the tree-line encroaching further up the mountainside.

which the hiking trail runs today. Similar geological formations are found between Mount Medstöten and Mount Korpflyet and between Mount Korpflyet and Mount Högfjället. The meltwater ran in channels between the ice, sculpting deep fissures, and also flowed in tunnels under the glaciers. Both these geological formations can be seen on the western slopes of Mount Gråsidan and Mount Högfjället.

Scientists have made exciting finds here in recent years, for example discovering that the boulder fields on the massif are far older than originally thought. Researchers previously believed that glacial movements had removed all loose-lying rock, but in some areas the glaciers had frozen against the ground and did not move when the ice above them shifted. As a result, the boulder fields at Sonfjället were left intact, and are the oldest geomorphological type known in Sweden today.

SKULESKOGEN

This multi-faceted national park on Sweden's highest stretch of coastline is famous for its stunning sea views. But first prize for stupendous scenery must go to the magnificent Slåttdalsskrevan, a ravine so deep that the people walking along it look like ants from above. From inside the ravine, the sheer rock faces rise up into a narrow slit of sky. The perfectly parallel walls and murky light create a dungeon-like atmosphere. At the top of the ravine, the Baltic Sea is in full view. Walk up to the edge of the precipice and peer down into the mine-shaft-like depths and you are guaranteed to go a little weak at the knees.

Bare granite rock extends in all directions, creating the feel of a weather-beaten island far out at sea. This sense is no mere figment of the imagination: Skuleskogen is a range of "till-capped" hills that once lay almost entirely under the sea. Like a group of islands, in other words.

The fertile moraine soil left behind by retreating glaciers on the protruding peaks is why dense forests now grow on the hilltops, giving them a capped appearance. The rock below the forests is rapakavi granite which the sea long ago stripped bare. The reddish rock is around one and a half billion years old (rapakavi is the oldest bedrock granite in Sweden) and takes its name from a Finnish word meaning rotten stone, referring to its tendency to erode into gravel.

Small patches of soil in some of the hillside crevices and cracks have allowed scattered trees to take root and grow. These stunted dwarf pines and birches are more reminiscent of a mountain landscape. The woodland is much denser at the bottom of the hills and in the ravines, where fine sediment once left behind by the sea provides fertile soil. Only the middle sections of the hills are bare, making them look very unusual from afar. Their rise from the sea was ultra-rapid – two hundred and eighty six metres over ten thousand four hundred years, which is a world record – and the waves fashioned mounds of shingle on the

Slåttdalsskrevan Ravine is forty metres deep and almost two hundred metres long. The seven-metre-wide gorge was once filled with brittle black diabase rock.

The rare old man's beard lichen can be found on spruce trees in damper areas of the national park. One of the longest lichens in the world, it can reach a length of ten metres. Old man's beard lichen has declined heavily in Sweden due to intensive forestry.

An uninterrupted view of the spectacular High Coast from Slåttdalsberget Hill. Lake Tärnättvattnen in the foreground lies one hundred and sixty-two metres above the Baltic Sea inlet of Näskefjärden to the north-east.

The channel between the mainland and the Tärnättholmarna islands is slowly disappearing due to isostatic land uplift, with the land currently rising at a rate of eighty centimetres per century. So shallow is the water that one can wade out to the islands. The national park's beaches are variously rocky, pebbly and sandy. The tall islands off the High Coast have wide coastal inlets. (Overleaf.)

beaches. The sea retreated as the land rose and these shingle fields today lie scattered through the forest. At the height of the Ice Age the inland ice was three kilometres thick here and so heavy that it created an eight-hundred-metre depression in the land. By the time the last glaciers had melted the land had recovered five hundred metres of this deficit, and the rebound process continues to this day.

Skuleskogen's outstanding isostatic land uplift geology fascinates scientists and is why UNESCO included the national park in the High Coast world heritage site. The High Coast comprises the national park and a stretch of coastline about eighty-five kilometres long in the Swedish province of Ångermanland by the Baltic Sea.

From Slåttdalsberget Hill, we take a section of the High Coast hiking trail, which runs for one hundred and thirty kilometres in all. We pass the ravine and the boulders and caves among which bandits once hid. New and old views combine as we descend a steep rocky staircase to a tiny plateau where the waters of Lake Tärnättvattnen lie smooth and tranquil. A sleeping cabin is available to visitors here. The trail leads from the lake down an even more impressive staircase to Salsviken Bay. This is one of Sweden's most aesthetic coastal paths, with sweeping views out to sea and distant offshore islands. The smooth rocks are easy to walk on, though steep at times. The occasional narrow and vertigo-inducingly steep chasm adds spice to the walk.

New impressions await. Like a beached whale offshore lies Mjältön, at two hundred and thirty six metres the country's highest island. Kälaviken is the national park's most sheltered beach and is popular with tourists during summer.

Man has inhabited Skuleskogen since ancient times. Burial mounds dating back to the early Bronze Age – when the sea level was thirty metres higher than it is today – can be found in the forest at Fjälludden. Seasonal livestock herding cabins existed for many hundreds of years in the national park, used by farmers to graze their animals in the forest during the summer months. A few of these cabins still survive at Näskebodarna, a private area inside the park, but of most only the foundations remain.

Human activity at Skuleskogen reached its height in the second half of the nineteenth century, when the saw mills of northern Sweden were crying out for timber. Almost all productive forest was logged and even rocky areas were stripped of harvestable trees, though today one can still find five-hundred-year-old pines that survived the cull. When the main wave of logging ended the woods were left to regenerate naturally. They have stood untouched for a century now and recovered a good measure of their former glory. Roughly half the forest is rocky pine forest; lush stands of spruce grow in the depressions and valleys.

The wildlife reflects the forest's high biological merit. Various woodpeckers breed and lynx prey on the deer and other game that thrive in the rolling terrain.

Skuleskogen is also the northernmost outpost for a number of southern tree species such as linden, sycamore and hazel – relics from a warmer climate. Conversely, some northern plants such as alpine catchfly, alpine saw-wort and the rare but easily recognised deer fern occur here far south of their usual ranges.

Slåttdalsberget Hill towers two hundred and eighty metres above the beach at Näskefjärden, with Slåttdalsskrevan Ravine appearing as a crack at the top of the photograph. The forest thins out as it rises up the hillside, exposing bare rocks on the ground beneath.

With its elegant plumes of lyme-grass, the sandy beach at Kälaviken is popular with bathers in summer. Just off the beach are an outdoor lavatory and windbreak. In winter the beach is usually deserted.

The spectacular view from the edge of Slåttdalsskrevan Ravine. Lake Tärnättvattnen is in the foreground and the Baltic Sea behind. (Overleaf.)

BJÖRNLANDET

Remote is an apt description of Björnlandet National Park. We drive for mile after mile along ever-narrower gravel roads through the empty forests of Västerbotten province. Here, in Sweden's sparsely populated north, the telltale signs of intensive forestry are all around, the landscape etched with pale patches of clear-felled forest and a warren-like network of roads. Until we reach Björnlandet. Human interference is conspicuous by its absence in this uninhabited vestige of Sweden's original, untamed taiga. The wildlife and landscape is as it was before the advent of modern forestry.

Until a national survey of pristine forest in the early 1980s, Björnlandet's attributes remained a well-kept secret. That isolated tracts between the provinces of Lappland and Ångermanland held a hidden remnant of pristine northern forest was news to the nature conservation authorities. After establishing that the area had no roads and was sufficiently large for national park status, the powers that be included Björnlandet in Sweden's first national parks programme. Formal inauguration came in 1991, with the official citation calling Björnlandet an outstanding example of a primeval forest with rolling boulder fields. There are current plans to extend the park to the south and east, an expansion that would see the protected area grow by forty percent.

The gravel road finally comes to a halt at Lake Angsjön, the only significant expanse of water in the park. An air of tranquillity hangs over the still surface, and the surrounding country holds a sense of promise. Tall rocky ridges envelope the lake, which lies in a bowl-shaped dip. The forest rises steeply up the slopes and on the crest we see high rocky precipices. At the end of the road, the national park's only walking trail leads up to Björnberget. Björnberget means Bear Rock in English and soon lives up to its name; fresh bear claw marks are clearly visible on a dead tree close to the trail. We become a little more watchful. Lynx also occur in the area, and wolverines pass through from time to time.

Björnlandet has many large boulders, including glacial erratics like these in Lake Angsjön. More extensive boulder fields can be found in the park's flatter areas.

The edible gypsy mushroom occurs widely in coniferous and birch forest nationwide, including at Björnlandet.

From the top of Björnberget one can see a clear difference between the national park's unbroken forest canopy and the clear-felled areas that pockmark the land outside the protected zone. The view also shows the rolling contours of the land.

Dusk falls on the mire beside Lake Ångsjön, where bog rosemary is in full bloom. The park's swampy areas are found between the rocky ridges.

The gradient becomes steeper towards the crag, which provides a magnificent viewpoint. Large boulders, ancient trees and storm-blown logs line the trail. A wealth of lichens cover the boulders: the whitish grey arctoparmelia lichen grows profusely on the upper parts of the rocks, making them glow like snowflakes in the murky light. Björnberget offers an excellent view of the eastern part of the park. The ridges that mark the northern perimeter are out of sight, and to the west lies a wilderness with no footpaths or trails down in a hollow that is also hidden from view.

The view from Björnberget is beautiful and striking. From here we see the national park in a wider context. Down below, Lake Ångsjön and the dense surrounding forest looks like a painting and contrasts sharply with the distant blue hills far to the south, where heavy logging has despoiled the landscape. If the truth be told, the national park itself suffered some logging in the early twentieth century, when ancient pines were cut down in the most easily accessible parts. Another small area was logged in 1951, and the log flumes along the stream leading from Lake Ångsjön testify to this period in the park's history. Local farmers also used to harvest sedge and grass from the bog for their animals, but none of these small vestiges of human activity detract at all from Björnberget's unspoiled environment.

Rich in dead trees and decaying wood, the old-growth forest at Björnberget is a haven for insects and fungi.

Pine is the commonest tree species, especially on the higher ground. The biggest and oldest trees are four hundred and fifty years old. The numerous charred pine trunks testify to forest fires, and indeed researchers have been able to identify several hundred blazes in the area, dating all the way back to the twelfth century. An absence of forest fires in more recent times has allowed spruce to gain a foothold. The oldest spruces are around two hundred and fifty years old and grow mainly in damper areas that are unlikely ever to have burnt.

We clamber among the boulders and blueberry bushes to explore Björnberget. A rocky ledge on the western side of the crag gives us a panoramic view. Rolling forest stretches as far as the eye can see. But even though it is early summer, we see little wildlife. The northern taiga is vast and empty, and animals always hard to spot.

The three-toed woodpecker is confined largely to spruce forest with deadwood and occurs at Björnlandet. This inhabitant of northern taiga forests has declined in Sweden due to deforestation and is now on the red list of threatened species.

The sedges growing in the mire north of Lake Angsjön were once cut with scythes for animal fodder. The rock in the background is named Jon Ersberget.

HAPARANDA SKÄRGÅRD

The boat journey from the mainland to Sandskär takes an hour. Out at sea, we pass scattered islets, clinging low to the horizon. Behind us, the mainland recedes and dissolves into strips. Light grey nimbus clouds fill the sky above, and beneath them the land crouches against the waterline. Though it is spring, the water still has its dark autumn hue. Space and emptiness reign: the occasional wooden cabin on the shoreline is the only sign of human life. Nestling among the bare rocks and islets are sun-warmed sandy beaches that offer the ultimate reward for those who come to explore this archipelago.

Haparanda Skärgård lies in the inner reaches of the Gulf of Bothnia, at the northernmost tip of the Baltic Sea. The sea is brackish, with a salt content of just two parts per thousand (sometimes less), and has the burnished, dusky colour of a freshwater lake. The sand and moraine islands are low-lying, the bays between them wide. Unlike most of Sweden's coastal archipelagos, the islets here are grouped not in dense clusters but are widely scattered. Land uplift means they are rising rapidly from the sea at a rate eighty-five millimetres per year – no less than eight-five centimetres per century. At this high-northern latitude, the light has an Arctic quality, and in summer the sun barely sets.

The islets have the freshness of youth and create an ever-changing landscape. A few thousand years ago this was unbroken sea, with barely a rock showing above the waterline. But the islets and sandbanks are constantly growing and gradually rising higher above the waves. We alight on a finger-like atoll pointing north on Sandskär, the largest island in the national park. The scenery here is reminiscent of another sandy national park, Gotska Sandön. And like its southern counterpart, Sandskär also emerged from the sea as a sandbar, eventually growing into an island. Heather and juniper flourish on the open ground. Pine trees stand dotted here and there.

The archipelago owes its shape to the moraine ridges left behind by the retreating ice sheet at the end of the Ice Age. Over time, the wind and

Lyme-grass binds the sand at Sandskär's northern tip, preventing erosion. Sea vetchling, with its mauve flowers, also helps to keep the sand in place. In the background are the islands of Korkea (to the left) and Kajava. Both are part of the national park.

Bird cherry also helps to stop sand from being scattered by the wind. The bird cherries of Sandskär grow in a unique creeping way and liven up the ground with their white blooms and exquisite scent.

The beach at Sandskär's northern tip is long and the waters offshore shallow. Weather-related factors mean the sea level in the innermost reaches of the Gulf of Bothnia can fluctuate by up to three metres.

The arctic tern is the national park's emblem. The species has increased throughout the Baltic and leaves its breeding grounds in August to start its long migration to its winter quarters in Antarctica.

A grey seal rests on a rock close to the island of Mali in the national park. Sometimes the seals lie here in groups. Ringed seals, a smaller species, occur south-east of Sandskär.

waves shifted the loose moraine and deposited it in new formations. Sand shifted to the northern sides of the islands and islets, unearthing large boulders on Sandskär's exposed southern coasts. The ridges themselves run from north-west to south-east and feature on nautical maps.

The national park includes the outermost islands of the Haparanda Sandskär archipelago, of which Sandskär is the largest. Seskar Furö, closer to the mainland, is covered largely by pinewoods. Though not as large as Sandskär, it is older (the rise of the land means that the outermost islands are the youngest). Various islands and islets, some bare sand and others covered by deciduous woods, also fall within the national park.

We leave Sandskär's long sandy beach and head out into a dry area of juniper bushes. Following the dunes southwards, we gaze out over the salt marsh on the eastern side. Boulders and rocks, some standing far out in the shallow water, perforate the flat expanse. When the sea recedes it exposes a muddy, sandy bottom. Farther out, the tiny island of Kajava, crowned by a small grove of trees, sits on the horizon. The island is an active fishing hamlet, and a few red fishermen's cabins stand beside the trees. The constant wind here eases the scourge of mosquitoes, an incessant and infuriating companion across much of northern Sweden in summer.

Moonlight over the sandbar on Sandskär's western shore. The sea, still cold in June, makes Malören, the most distant island, shimmer like a mirage on the horizon. Situated just outside the national park, Malören has a fishing harbour and a lighthouse that has stood since 1851. (Previous page.)

The shy red-breasted merganser in courtship display at Sandskär. The species still breeds here but its numbers have fallen sharply in Sweden in the last century for unknown reasons. Sandskär is an Eldorado for birdwatchers – a gateway through which millions of migrating birds pass each year. Two hundred and thirty-one species have been recorded and around fifty breed regularly.

A flock of whooper swans resting in one of Sandskär's bays, probably en route to their breeding grounds in the bogs of Lapland. The island of Malören lies eight kilometres out to sea.

There is no denying that Sandskär is a haven for mosquitoes. For all their bloodthirsty nuisance value to humans, they are a vital food for many birds.

Gnarled pines in the dense pine forest in the centre of Sandskär. Black and willow grouse occur side by side here, and in this part of the island large aspens form a wood all of their own. The birch trees here are short and stunted like mountain birches.

In the far distance we see the Finnish coast, where smoke spews from a steelworks. To the west, we see only the horizon, but the visibility is so good that a white pall of smoke from the steelworks in Luleå, seventy kilometres away on the Swedish side, can be seen in the air above the skyline.

We head for the centre of the island and arrive at East and West Stadium, two flat heath-like areas surrounded by a protective cordon of sand dunes nearly twenty metres high – the highest on the island. The wind is the master sculptor here, though a dense pine forest has managed to establish itself in the centre of the island.

The sand in the southern part of Sandskär is coarser and topped by stones. The vegetation shrinks into small clumps. We reach Kumpula, an old fishing hamlet with a harbour wall where boats can moor. Men would come here in former times to hunt seals on the spring ice or fish for salmon and herring. The salmon was sent to Stockholm, while the herring was the local staple. In those times, people lived on Sandskär for a season and then abandoned the island during winter.

PIELJEKAISE

From the slopes of Mount Pieljekaise the view is panoramic and the magnificent scenery truly worthy of national park status. Gently rolling forests of mountain birch unfurl into the distance, the sea of green interspersed with lakes and pools glinting like gemstones among the trees. In the distance lie bogs and mires, and beyond them mountain ridges form a jagged backdrop against the sky. In the other direction, beside us, the fells extend like a flat plain.

This protected area sits between vast coniferous forests to the east and high mountains to the west. No signs of civilisation are visible: this is a true wilderness. Its history as a national park dates back to 1905, when the regional crown forester, Gustav Tjäder, wrote a personal recommendation to the Royal Swedish Academy of Sciences' nature conservation committee, which had invited proposals for the country's first national parks. "I cannot avoid mentioning the presence of rather remarkable forest meadows in a part of these tracts," Tjäder wrote. "The location is south of Mount Peljekaise … "

The crown forester had visited the area and been fascinated by the upland birch trees "which recall our everyday fruit trees". Clearly, Tjäder had rather limited experience of the mountains because there is nothing unusual about the birchwoods at Pieljekaise: mountain birches almost always look like fruit trees. All the same, the government of the day responded to his appeal to preserve the area's forest meadows and declared two hundred hectares of Pieljekaise a national park in 1909.

Another forester was given the task of marking out the border, and he reported back to his superiors that the protected area was too small. A couple of years later the government approved an extension of the park to the boundaries that still apply today.

Awareness of Sweden's nature and wildlife was understandably sketchier a century ago compared to today. The areas included in the park zone were selected on no particular systematic or scientific basis. But in Pieljekaise's case, the decisions made back then have proved to be the

The midnight sun illuminates the fells east of Mount Pieljekaise. Blue-green osier bushes cling tight to the flat plain. Around a quarter of the national park is above the tree-line.

Elk find plentiful grazing in the lush birchwoods. The animals move down into the coniferous forests when snow blankets the mountains in winter. Brown bear and lynx also appear in the national park from time to time.

Alpine meadow birch forest extends from the southern slope of Mount Pieljekaise and is the richest habitat in the national park. Globeflower, crane's-bill and red campion provide a splash of vivid colour in these magnificent natural herb gardens.

right ones. Gustav Tjäder noted that the birchwoods were untouched by human hand, other than the Sami reindeer herders who would fell trees for firewood and tent poles. The Sami, after all, had inhabited the area for many hundreds of years. Aside from this very limited human impact, Pieljekaise's birch forests are untouched and fully merit the protection they enjoy today. Indeed, the montane woodland here is among the most pristine of its type in the country. It is an important biotope on account of its size, sandwiched between the coniferous forest belt and the high fells, and is characteristic of the Swedish mountains. In most mountain regions around the world, deciduous trees do not grow up to the tree-line.

The birch trees that grow in the Swedish mountains are considered an evolutionary form of the downy birch and can grow in lower temperatures than coniferous species. Downy birch forests can vary enormously in character, some creating an airy park-like atmosphere while others shift from dense tropical-like jungle to sparse Arctic bushland. The Kungsleden, or Royal Trail, that passes through the park offers a good insight into this variation. Beneath Mount Pieljekaise the trail enters a natural garden of tall flowers and ferns, but for the most part the path runs through dry birchwoods that are of meagre botanical interest yet kind to the eye with

their lush greenery. Downy birch forest is unusual in that it consists of just one species – a natural monoculture. Occasional willows, rowans and aspens grow here and there but the downy birch is king. The forest is light and airy, almost like a herb garden, though in some years infestations of the autumnal moth larva strip the branches bare and reduce the woods to leafless skeletons. One such infestation occurred in 1955–57 at Lake Aleb Tjallasjaure. Repeated attacks in successive years can kill the trees and turn the forest into a ghost-like desert.

Lake Gaskka-Bieljávrre is the largest area of water in the eastern part of the national park. Here the dense birchwoods stretch for miles and miles, relieved only by lakes and waterside marshes. The hunched out-line of Mount Krappesvare shows in the background.

Pieljekaise National Park seen in profile from Lake Bajep Juhtas to the east. The name Pieljekaise means "ear mountain" in the Sami language. Reaching an altitude of eleven hundred metres, the mountain towers above the surrounding scenery. (Overleaf.)

MUDDUS

The hiking trail leads to the observation tower at Muddusluobbal. We have reached this spot after passing thundering waterfalls, waterlogged marshes, glistening lakes and myriad trees – pine and spruce, some thick and others slender in girth – sparsely dotted across the flat land. The tower stands in the middle of nowhere, surrounded by the lonely taiga: a virgin landscape that we quickly take to our hearts. Size is important – the air of distance and the untouched. Wind and fire, not the logger's saw, are the guiding hand in primeval forests. Nature taking its own course.

The word taiga comes from Mongolian or Turkic and refers to the vast belt of coniferous forest stretching from the Bering Strait across Siberia to Scandinavia. All coniferous forest in Sweden is technically taiga, but I suspect the word means something a little extra to most of us. In our mind's eye we see taiga as vast forest wildernesses punctuated with empty boglands and a low covering of twigs and brushwood. All these ingredients are found at Muddus, where it is easy to get lost in the backwoods if you wander off from the trail. The name Muddus is a Sami word meaning "the just-right country" or "the country more or less".

Muddus's gushing rivers, whose white water and currents make log rafting too dangerous, epitomise its untamed beauty. Here in this inaccessible wilderness, a settler called Israel Jacobsson once built a farm in the mid-1800s, growing potatoes and harvesting fodder from the mires for his animals. He made a home on the eastern shore of Muddusjaure, the largest lake in the area, but abandoned the place in 1909. In the 1920s a forester by the name of Edvard Wibeck began campaigning for Muddus to be made a national park and in 1935 made a radio speech urging Sweden's forest owners to preserve the country's remaining virgin forests. Wibeck was a little ahead of his time and it was not until 1942 that Muddus became a national park – the first for more than a decade.

Today, this great expanse of primeval forest is a national legacy. Research has shown that wildlife species which depend on untouched forest are commoner in Muddus than in the managed forests outside the national park.

Måskoskårså, thought to have been formed by glacial meltwater during the late Ice Age, has a special microclimate that is warmer than the surrounding area. Various unusual plants grow here. The vertigo-inducing ravine is best observed from the hiking trail that runs for its two-kilometre length.

Whooper swans are a familiar sight nowadays in Muddus but were rare in Sweden in the 1940s when the national park was established.

From Muddusluobbal we see north-west towards Lake Muddusjaure, half-hidden behind the forest, and beyond to Mount Lilvuosmo, which rises to a height of six hundred and ten metres (overleaf).

Capercaillie and pine marten both have healthy populations. Brown bear and lynx occur regularly, and wolverines pass through from time to time. Golden eagle, peregrine falcon and eagle owl – three birds of prey all sensitive to human disturbance – breed in the park.

Spruce dominates the forest in the central and western parts, where the flora is interesting and calypso orchid can be found in damp areas. Pine takes over on the barren moors in the east and south, and here stands Sweden's oldest known pine tree, a specimen that is more than seven hundred years old. Despite its grand old age, the tree is surprisingly unimpressive in dimension at less than half a metre across and sixteen metres high. Trees grow extremely slowly in these far-northern climes and the rings on a trunk are densely packed.

In the same area grows another pine which scientists have dated back to 1490 and which stands on a spot ravaged by fire in 2006. The researchers who analysed the tree found evidence of five different fires, the oldest two dating back to the seventeenth century and the most recent in 1933. The latter blaze is thought to have been ignited by sparks from a bonfire in the hamlet of Sarkavare just outside the national park. The most recent fire at Muddus was in 2006 and probably caused by lightning. It raged for nearly three weeks, devastating three hundred hectares of land.

The Muddus River flows quietly beneath towering rock faces. A long stretch of whitewater rapids awaits little further downstream.

The Muddus falls are a spectacular sight. The lake at their base marks the start of the six-kilometre River Muddus canyon.

However, fires play an important role in nature and are vital for biological diversity, with many species of animal and plant (especially fungi, lichens and insects) depending on charred wood and ground for their existence.

Muddus is largely flat, with a central plain encircled by a ring of well spaced, tree-clad and often conical monadnocks (rocky hills) – a geological formation that covers large parts of northern Scandinavia. The rock is ancient granite and gneiss bedrock. The wide expanses and serene peaks combine with the open boglands and lakes to impart tranquility to the mosaic-like landscape. We gain a good view from Mount Sörstubba, the highest point in the national park at six hundred and fifty-eight metres above sea level. The peak is easily reached from the E45 highway, which skirts the park's northern boundary. From the summit we see a patchwork of forest, mires and lakes stretching for miles and miles and not the faintest sign of human presence. To the east, the view sweeps over an empty wilderness without houses, meadows, roads or mobile phone masts. But looking north one can see the town of Gällivare in the middle distance.

From above, the boglands are grid-like, with long upraised strips of brushwood and grass separated by marshy streaks of different sizes.

Plentiful deadwood provides a rich environment for fungi and insects. In most areas of the national park the trees are well spaced, making the forest easily accessible – and easy to get lost in. Blueberry and lingonberry bushes grow beneath the canopy. (Previous page.)

In winter the forest becomes inaccessible and deathly quiet. Here in the River Muddus Gorge the snow lies a metre deep. Not even a raven cries.

The River Muddus is ice-bound in the depths of winter, though a few open pools provide an eye-catching contrast between the brown waters and pearl-white snow.

In summer, they are almost impassable and teem with mosquitoes and biting black flies. They are easier to negotiate with skis in winter (but not snow scooters, which are banned within the park boundaries).

The hiking trail passes Muddus's precipitous ravines. Running for ten kilometres to the Lule River valley, they are the park's most stunning sight. The most dramatic is Måskoskårså, a dry gorge one hundred metres deep and filled with boulders. Another carries the waters of the River Muddus, which plunges in two waterfalls forty-two metres into twin ravines and then flows for a short distance quietly past high rock faces before rushing into rapids that run for nearly six kilometres to its mouth in the Lule River.

The Muddus taiga as seen from Mount Sörstubba, the highest peak. An autumn shower sweeps over the yellowing bogland, which covers around forty percent of the national park.

The River Muddus Gorge gradually widens and becomes less steep as the river continues its course through the national park.

STORA SJÖFALLET

Sweden's third-largest national park arouses conflicting emotions. For Stora Sjöfallet is a place of two extremes, combining awe-inspiring mountain scenery with environmental destruction. I ask myself whether we should concentrate on the nature and wildlife that remains, or on what has been lost. Either way, we must never forget what happened here, the site of the biggest ever assault on Sweden's natural environment. Once one of Europe's most unique waterfalls, Stora Sjöfallet was sacrificed to meet growing energy needs. A hydroelectric dam was built upstream to create a huge reservoir that reduced the falls to a shadow of their former grandeur. Construction work began in the late 1920s and took more than fifty years to complete, as roads and power lines gradually invaded this corner of wilderness. Areas used by generations of Sami reindeer herders to graze their animals were eventually flooded, and numerous wild animals lost their natural habitats.

Much has been written about the destruction of this unique waterfall, described as "an entire landscape of falling water" by one impressed visitor in 1913. Today, there is no escaping the fact that its destruction continues to cast a long shadow over the national park. And yet, the parts not affected by the dam remain among the most beautiful mountain areas in the country. This is the contradictory essence of Stora Sjöfallet National Park.

The dam turned a necklace of pristine lakes into an artificial inland sea now known as the Akkajaure Reservoir. It is north of here, at Vakkotavare, that we begin our walk into the national park. We start by taking the Kungsleden, or Royal Trail, up a steep mountain slope. On reaching the top of the ridge a magnificent mountain panorama stretches out before us.

Stora Sjöfallet National Park can be seen as two halves, one north and one south of the reservoir, that meet in the east of the protected zone. The southern half is highly varied, with mountain birch forests, desolate fells and Sweden's most beautiful mountains, the Akka massif, as the icing on the cake. This majestic chain of peaks, known as the Queen of

A tussock of roseroot growing beside the River Mávgojåhkå, with the Akka massif in the background. Between the river and valley is the Akkajaure Reservoir, invisible to the eye from this angle. Roseroot is a medicinal plant believed to have sedative properties.

Willow grouse breed in the birch forests by the Akkajaure Reservoir. Unlike the closely related ptarmigan, which favours high altitudes, the willow grouse lives below the tree-line. Both species occur in the national park, though their numbers fluctuate from year to year.

Mount Lulep Gierkav has a steep north-east face with large scree slopes below. The peak can be seen from the eastern section of the road that passes through the national park. Lake Langas, in the foreground, is still untouched and one of a series of lakes that are the source for the Great Lule River.

The fells east of Stora Sjö-fallet National Park at first light, seen from the top of Mount Sluggá. Below this peak, once sacred to the Sami people, lies Lake Pietsaure, and behind it, in morning shadow, is the south face of Mount Lulep Gierkav. (Overleaf.)

Lapland, lies in splendid isolation in the western corner of the park. The southern half of the park adjoins Sarek National Park and there has been talk of merging the two into a single large park south of the Akkajaure Reservoir.

Kallaktjåkkå, a high mountain ridge, dominates the northern part of the national park. Though gently rounded, the peak is high and icebound on the upper reaches. We walk down it onto a flat fell from where the views to the west and south are breathtaking. Suddenly we notice an optical illusion: the valley and its hydroelectric dam that divides the national park are hidden from view, making it look as if the northern and southern parts of the park connect together as one. The high fells seem to stretch unbroken for twenty kilometres or more to the spectacular alpine peaks of Sarek to the south. I hardly know whether to laugh or cry. From here, the scenery boasts all the finest attributes of the Swedish mountains: unbroken panoramas, freedom, stunning alpine peaks and fascinating bird life.

And yet this is a wounded area. Clumps of yellow mountain saxifrage and mountain avens lift the spirits, while a flock of long-tailed ducks swims in one of the numerous lakes. The Akka massif stands proudly beyond them. This compact alpine massif means "old woman" in the Sami language and was in the past regarded as sacred by the reindeer-herding Sami, who have existed here for thousands of years. Akka and Kallaktjåkkå both have a number of glaciers, though these have receded dramatically in the last century, as they have at Nieras, the third of the national park's three main massifs.

There is a visitor's centre at Vietas, close to the sad trickle that is now Stora Sjöfallet. The one hundred and fifty kilometre-long road built to provide access to the hydroelectric power station passes here, and the River Viedasädno and its deep valley extends to the north-east. The Viedasädno has also been dammed for hydroelectric power, but I try to focus on the positives. The scenery around Vietas is impressive, with old pinewoods in the deep valley. At an altitude of just four hundred metres, this is one of the most impressive forests in the entire Swedish mountains, with numerous old trees and twisted deadwood. Lying beneath a dramatic backdrop of rocky precipices, this pristine habitat is readily accessible and easily explored on foot. Vietas has also been designated as the site for a centre for the Laponia world heritage site, which as well as Stora Sjöfallet also includes the Sjaunja nature reserves and Sarek, Padjelanta and Muddus national parks.

The old pine forest in the valley at Vietas. Many of the trees have stood for two hundred years, while the oldest specimens are around five hundred years old.

A reindeer herder's cabin by the River Gappestjåhkkå, bathed in evening sunlight. The Sami village of Sörkai-tum has reindeer grazing rights in the north of the national park and Sirka Sami village uses the southern parts.

The night sky reflected in Lake Mávogojávre in the shadow of the Kallaktjåkkå mountain ridge. The name Kallaktjåkkå means "cold mountain" in the Sami language.

It is mid-June and the ice on Lake Nuortab Átjek is melting. The rounded peaks overlooking the lake are arranged like burial mounds. Mount Stuor Átjek, far right, rises to a height of one thousand three hundred and eighty metres. This southern part of the national park is remote and seldom visited by hikers. (Overleaf.)

SAREK

Stillness is a clear winter's day in Sarek when the wind has died. Piercing cold and desolate scenery create a timeless landscape that has looked this way since prehistoric times. A thick blanket of pure white snow dampens all sound, the tall mountains forming a wall that shuts out distant civilised worlds. Motor vehicles are prohibited in the national park and those of us who make our way here, with only skis for transport, are guests in a foreign and pristine world. Unmatched in Sweden for its emptiness, Sarek is accessible in winter only to those who defy the risks involved. Arctic temperatures and the remote, inhospitable terrain make this a dangerous place. A winter's visit is a tough and demanding adventure – and a journey back to our roots. That a wilderness of this calibre still exists in Europe is truly fantastic.

And then there is summer – three to four short snowless months – when Sarek is transformed, its valleys brimming with life. We see birds returning to breed, plants absorbing the round-the-clock daylight, big game moving cautiously over the fells, and hikers exploring this breathtaking wilderness.

There is nowhere wilder in Sweden than Sarek – nowhere that can match the magnificence of its scenery, with its glaciers, rivers, mountains, forests, deltas and animal life. Sarek is the very incarnation of a national park, with its brutal, towering mountain peaks, some sharp and some rounded, and hundreds of glaciers. Lush vegetation carpets the valley floors during summer, while the high passes become stony deserts and the steep mountainsides of black amphibolite plunge into the valleys. It is almost as if the topography has been landscaped. A dozen large massifs with high peaks and narrow ridges form contours that resemble blocks on an urban street map. Between them lie valleys with narrow corridors and wide avenues, a labyrinthine world to excite the curiosity of any hiker.

The process of erosion is unusually evident at Sarek. It is as if nature is giving us a geology lesson. When hiking through the long Rapadalen

A climber stands atop Mount Tvillingryggen, with Mount Bálgattjåhkå – Sweden's eleventh highest peak at just over two thousand metres – in the background. Freezing fog surrounds the mountains in winter, creating a swirl of patterns and concealing the mountainsides.

Perfectly adapted to Sarek's harsh winter climate, the hardy ptarmigan is the main prey of the rare gyrfalcon, several pairs of which nest in the national park. Ptarmigan numbers fluctuate from year to year.

Other than at first light during the short summer, the north face of Mount Sarektjåhkkå spends the year in permanent shade. The north peak, to the left, is extremely steep and the main peak, to the right, is Sweden's third highest at two thousand and eighty-nine metres. The cartographer G.W. Bucht climbed it in 1879 by following the western ridge from the right.

The Rapa delta, where the River Ráphaädno flows into Lake Laitaure, lies outside the national park but is due to become part of the protected zone in the future. Since the nineteenth century the delta has been part of two homesteads at Aktse, to the left of Lake Laitaure. The photograph was taken from Mount Nammásj. (Overleaf.)

Valley we pass three large deltas, created by silt once dislodged from the mountain tops by shifting ice and transported here by Sarek's rivers. These are decorative environments, with their grey sandbars, blackish mudflats, green fens, silvery sallows, orange iron sediment, and turquoise channels and lagoons. Seen from the mountaintops above, the deltas look like a freshly painted oil canvas.

The abundance of silt makes the valley soil highly fertile. In summer, Rapadalen Valley is like a luxuriant jungle hemmed in between walls of rock. Here the undergrowth is so dense as to make the forest almost impenetrable. But though impassable to humans, these areas provide plentiful grazing and are favoured by large mammals. So rich is the vegetation that Sarek's elks are as large as their cousins in Alaska, the bulls awe-inspiring with their massive antlers. Brown bears, wolverines and lynx all occur in the deep birch forests of the valleys of Rapadalen and Njåtjosvagge. Coniferous forest grows in the southern part of the national park, but Sarek is first and foremost an alpine environment – especially in the north. Barren fells, bare rock and snow and ice cover ninety percent of the national park, a few large lakes adding a splash of blue to the rugged landscape.

There is a sense of the eternal about this inaccessible wilderness, though that is a relative notion in geological terms. Sarek's mountaintops formed four hundred million years ago from rock that once lay below a western sea. Erosion soon began to take its toll, with layer after layer of rock peeled away by the elements, only for the bedrock to rise again to create a new alpine plain and start a new cycle. And so it continued down the ages. The mountains of today are not the first to have stood here, merely the youngest. But at ten million years old they deserve the eternal moniker.

By comparison, Sarek's glaciers are mere infants. For warm periods after the Ice Age there was no ice here at all. Thereafter the climate became colder and large glaciers formed from the falling snow. The ice sheets remained thick from the seventeenth century until the early twentieth century, but since then have been in retreat. Perhaps emissions of greenhouse gases have accelerated the natural process of climate change? Whatever the causes, Sarek's glaciers are certainly shrinking.

Not until the 1880s did the first cartographers visit these remote wilds. Axel Hamberg, professor of geography at Uppsala University, conducted surveys here a century ago after first hiking through the area in 1895. The national park has never been inhabited, though Sami reindeer herders have visited the area frequently down the ages and for a short while in the seventeenth century a small mine was operational. The prospectors hoped to dig for silver but found mostly lead, which they transported on reindeer sleighs to a smelting cabin in the village of Kvikkjokk south of the national park.

Aktse, an idyllic farmstead on the edge of the forest just outside the national park, was built in the mid-nineteenth century. We reach it via the popular Royal Trail that passes this corner of Sarek. From here, we see the shark-fin outline of Mount Skierffe against the skyline. The area at its base is sacred to the indigenous Sami people, for whom Sarek has always been special.

Many hikers make the trek to the summit to witness the most vertiginous view in Sweden: right below your feet, seven hundred metres down, lies the Rapa delta. Beyond, the rugged peaks of Sarek line up into the distance.

"This is Sweden's widest alpine vista and compares with Norway's Mount Jotunheimen in area, height and magnificence," wrote Axel Hamberg in 1922.

In the other direction, far to the east, the view sweeps over waves of forested ridges towards the Lapland interior. We also see the glinting surface of the Tjaktjajaure Reservoir, created just outside the national park in the 1960s as part of a hydroelectric dam project. This venture resulted in a small part of Sarek being submerged under water, but in return the national park was extended southwards to include Pårek, an area of lakes and bogs with a rich bird life.

Mount Bielloriehppe rises one thousand two hundred metres above Rapaselet in the fifty-kilometre-long Rapadalen Valley, which bisects Sarek. The River Ráhpaädno in the foreground carries vast quantities of glacial silt that accumulates in the delta.

Huge elk can be seen in Rapadalen Valley. These spectacular animals migrate to summer pastures up in the fells, spending the winter in the lowland forests.

A ray of midnight sun falls on Suottasjjiegna, one of the largest glaciers in the national park. The peaks of Mount Såltatjåhkkå tower over the ice, which has receded alarmingly fast in recent decades due to climate change. Given current concern over global warming, the Sarek glaciers have become an important subject of scientific study. (Overleaf.)

Reindeer feeding on lichens at an altitude of fifteen hundred metres. At this height, they can graze in peace from mosquitoes and biting flies.

At eight hundred and twenty-three metres above sea level, the cube-shaped Mount Nammasj stands sentry-like over the delta landscape of eastern Sarek. The mountain has a hard granite shell that protects it from erosion and is known in geological terms as a butte.

The April sun rises from behind the north face of Mount Sarektjåhkkå. Sarek is a desolate place in winter.

Lake Bierikjávrre, one of the national park's large lakes, seen from Mount Sarva-tjåhkkå. Its vivid turquoise colours come from sunlight illuminating particles of glacial silt suspended in the water.

Meltwater from the Alep Basstajiegna glacier has carved out a channel in the ice. In summer Sarek's glaciers are covered in water which stands in pools on the ice and can create treacher-ous chasms for those who venture onto them.

PADJELANTA

Padjelanta, the largest and most remote of all Sweden's national parks, is a place of grandiose vistas and wide open spaces. Its rolling alpine plains and expanses of open water exude a unique magic. The lakes here are among the biggest in the Swedish fells and the mountain peaks mainly low and gently sloping. A sensual landscape, one might say – and illuminated by a backdrop of light that sets its own special seal on the surroundings. For a Swedish mountain region, the national park is unusually open and accessible, its scenery inviting meditation. Every time I visit Padjelanta I find myself reflecting on life.

Padjelanta is made for the walker and contrasts with neighbouring Sarek National Park, whose dramatic terrain is more suited to the adventurer. The two parks border each other but differ considerably. Where Sarek boasts alpine peaks, valleys teeming with elk and game, glaciers, a large river delta and forests, Padjelanta is a botanist's paradise with magnificent panoramic views, slower flowing rivers, softer bedrock, a richer birdlife and almost no forest at all.

The name Padjelanta comes from the Lule Sami word Badjelánnda meaning "the higher land" – an apt description. Remains of ancient Sami culture have been found throughout the park. Historians are not sure how long the reindeer-herding Sami have inhabited the area, but in all likelihood they have been here for thousands of years. Certainly, Padjelanta is an important place in the Sami culture and the government noted this in 1962 when it declared the area a national park, with the park management plan explicitly stressing the need to take special account of reindeer herders' needs.

When Padjelanta became part of the UNESCO world heritage site Laponia its importance to the Sami nation, Sápmi, became even more entrenched.

Padjelanta's rolling fells are valuable reindeer grazing land, while its lakes teem with fish. The reindeer-herding Sami lived as nomads until the middle of the last century, accompanying their animals on their seasonal

A clump of glacier crow-foot growing at a height of fourteen hundred metres beside Ålmåjjiegna, Sweden's second largest glacier, in the south-west corner of the national park. Glacier crow-foot grows at higher altitude than any other vascular plant.

The Norwegian lemming occurs throughout Sweden's mountains and is a so-called indicator species that is crucial to other species' survival. Lemmings occur in huge numbers during "lemming years", enabling birds of prey and the rare Arctic fox to rear more young than usual.

This unnamed pool south of Oarjep Rissávárre in the east of the national park is in the middle of a roadless tract that measures one hundred kilometres across and is the most remote spot in all of Sweden.

Sarek's peaks reflected in a small lake in the east of Padjelanta National Park. Carl Linnaeus passed this spot when returning from Norway during his Lapland odyssey in 1732.

Cotton grass growing beside a small mere south of Staloluokta, with Mount Sulitelma in the background. (Overleaf.)

migrations. Down the ages the national park has served as summer pasture for reindeer, and still serves this purpose today. The Sami herders lived close to their animals during summer, but the park has had no permanent residents for the last few centuries at least. That said, Mount Silbbatjåhkkå on Padjelanta's southern perimeter witnessed a boom in 1657 with the discovery of silver deposits. A mine was built and employed a hundred people before closing thirty or so years later. The remains of the old shafts can still be seen today.

Padjelanta's cultural history has left little imprint on its rugged wilderness. Here, nature's laws have ruled free from the hand of human interference. Relentless westerly winds buffet the park during the long, harsh winter months.

The Atlantic Ocean is not far away, just across the Norwegian border, and storms are frequent. And yet on warm summer days there is no place in the Swedish mountains more serene than Padjelanta. The national park is popular with foreign visitors, who are enthusiastic users of its hiking trails. Perhaps the soft contours of Padjelanta's scenery are what attracts them.

The bedrock of brittle mountain slate shapes the landscape and also explains the park's diverse flora. The northern and western areas have large quantities of highly alkaline serpentinite, a rock containing high concentrations of heavy metals. Botanic rarities can be found on serpentinite outcrops. Mount Jiegnáffo, the highest peak in the national park at 1,836 metres, is known for its plant life. The extremely rare Robbins' cinquefoil, first found by Swedish botanist Sten Selander in the 1940s, grows here. Selander, who was also a well known novelist, studied Padjelanta's plant life and was an heir to the tradition of the legendary botanist Carl Linnaeus, who visited Padjelanta during his journey to Lapland in 1732. Linnaeus made copious notes on the flora of this remote, and in those days highly inaccessible, region. L.J. Montin, a prominent Linnaeus disciple, visited the central parts of the national park in 1749 and stood at the exact spot by Lake Virihaure where his mentor had stood seventeen years before. The lake lies in the very heart of the park and on its shores is Staloluokta, a Sami camp which existed even back in Linnaeus' time. The popular Padjelanta Trail passes here and there is a Sami camp, chapel and a tourist sleeping cabin. Mount Unna Dijdder, which overlooks Staloluokta, is known for its unusually rich plant life, including montane birch forest.

The waterfall at Såjåsjávrre forms the park's current boundary. The Mount Sorjostjåhkå shows in the background, on the other side of the Norwegian border.

The River Stálojåhkå rushes into Lake Virihaure at the Staloluokta Sami camp. An angler chances his luck in the lake. The commonest fish is char, which Sami fishermen catch using nets.

A blue light over Lake Virihaure on a summer's night. The lake, the fifth deepest in the country at one hundred and thirty-eight metres, gives Padjelanta a special radiance.

Just outside the park's southern border is Sulitelma, part of the Laponia world heritage site and an extensive alpine massif bisected by the Swedish-Norwegian border. On the Swedish side we find two of the country's largest glaciers.

When proposals to build hydroelectric dams on Padjelanta's rivers were first mooted in the late 1950s, Sten Selander led a campaign to preserve the area as a wilderness. In 1961, nature conservation organisations signed a pact with energy industry officials that led to Padjelanta being declared a national park. The higher land was saved for posterity. Now, several decades later, plans are afoot to extend the park's boundaries and protect even more of this unique mountain wilderness.

The River Låddejåhkå runs from Sarek in the east to its mouth in Lake Vastenjaure in the west. The popular Padjelanta Trail passes here and Mount Guopher and Mount Lanjektjåhkkå stand to the left and right respectively.

The undulating landscape of central Padjelanta seen from Mount Nijak in the north of Sarek National Park. Snow still covers much of the ground even in early July.

Lake Vastenjaure is the second largest body of water in Padjelanta. The southern shore is flat, while the northern shore at Aralåbddå has rocky outcrops and a rich flora. (Overleaf.)

ABISKO

Abisko, in Sweden's wild far north, is one of the country's oldest and best-known national parks, a place of outstanding beauty. The excellent climate is another attraction: Abisko, which lies in a mountain rain shadow, is one of the sunniest spots in the country. And the stunning landscape is not easily forgotten. In Roman mythology, a *genius loci* was a spirit that protected a place. These days, we talk about that indefinable atmosphere which certain landscapes and countryside possess. To me, Abisko has its own genius loci: the rich birch forest, the elegant contours of the land and the tranquil waters of Lake Torneträsk. But most of all it is the sum of what the eye sees and the heart feels that has the profoundest effect. Abisko always instils a desire to return.

A wide valley with mountain birch forest runs through the national park. The name Abisko comes from the language of the indigenous Sami people and means "sea forest", perhaps because the Atlantic Ocean is just a short distance away across the Norwegian border, or because the Sami people saw Lake Torneträsk as an inland sea. The lake is the largest in the Scandinavian mountains and, seen from Abisko, is a full ten kilometres across. However, only a tiny section of the lake – the mouth of the River Abiskojåkka and its delta, plus a small island – actually fall within the national park. The River Abiskojåkka gushes like an artery through the valley, bringing with it crystal-clear water from Lake Ábeskojávri to the impressive gorge at its mouth. It was this ravine and the botanically rich birch forests that prompted state geologist Fredrik Svenonius to recommend that Abisko be made a national park in 1907. Two years later, Parliament granted formal approval.

The park boundary follows the western mountainsides to Ábeskojávri, a sizeable lake in a basin-like valley inside the park. By the water stands the precipitous Giron, a steep crag with black slopes. To the east, the rolling birch forest unfolds and here Abisko's boundary runs as an invisible straight line beneath the greenery.

The old railway line from 1902 to Kiruna iron mine and the E10 highway

A cable car runs to the top of Mount Njulla. The peak gives a magnificent view of Lapporten (Gateway of Lappland), the most famous landmark in the Swedish mountains. Lapporten, which is just outside the national park, is known as Cuonjávággi in the Sami language and attracts artists from far and wide.

Abisko is known as the garden of the Swedish mountains for its rich flora, which thrives on the calcareous soil. The bluntleaved orchid is the most famous plant species. The moors beside the River Abiskojåkka are popular with walkers and are home to Lapland rhododendron, yellow alpine milkvetch, fragrant orchid and, as in the photograph, yellow mountain saxifrage.

The River Abiskojåkka widens and gains force at the old marble quarry a few kilometres south of the gorge. The crystal-clear water is due to the absence of glaciers in the catchment area.

The floral carpet above the tree-line on Mount Njulla is among the most dazzling in the country. Here we see crane's-bill, globeflower and red campion. Mount Njulla's plant life has been the subject of botanic study since the Abisko Scientific Research Station was founded a century ago. The centre, run by the Royal Swedish Academy of Sciences, enjoys a strong international reputation.

pass through the north of the park, providing easy access for tourists and other visitors. Many Abisko aficionados, I among them, protested when the highway was built in the 1980s. We thought the road would destroy Abisko's genius loci, though that gloomy view has since changed. In any case, you can never turn the clock back, and we still visit the national park.

Beside the road and railway line, the Abisko tourist hotel enjoys a commanding view over the Abisko "Alps", as they are known locally. (Although high, these gracious mountain peaks are, in fact, not like the rugged Alps at all but altogether smoother and more rounded.) The hotel marks the start – and finish – of Kungsleden, or the Royal Trail, a hiking trail that runs for four hundred and twenty kilometres through Lapland. The trail got its name in the 1930s and at Abisko follows the River Abiskojåkka through the birchwoods. The forest in the valley is dry and contains some unusual treeless patches that have attracted scientific interest. In winter, the snow is not as deep as would be expected this far north, causing frost to penetrate far beneath the surface, and it is thought that the patches may be treeless for this reason. Ground movements and frost certainly make the land inhospitable to plant life. Abisko is a national park where the interests of science and tourism go hand in hand.

Reindeer herders from Gabna, a Sami village, shepherd their animals from Mount Giron down to lower ground, where the calves will be marked. Reindeer herds pass Abisko every year en route from their summer pastures to their winter feeding grounds. (Previous page.)

The rock-faces of Abiskojåkka Gorge stand twenty metres high and perpendicular to the ground. A gap in the bedrock reveals the different geological types. The Swedish mountains consist of multiple nappes of rock lying in layers on top of each other.

A creamy, magnesium-rich rock known as dolomite lines the base of the Abisko gorge. Dolomite is used as an ornamental stone and has been quarried in a few places along the River Abiskojåkka.

The limestone-loving elegant sunburst lichen adds a splash of vivid colour at the head of Abiskojåkka Gorge. The slopes of Mount Njulla, where scientists study changes in the tree line, are visible in the background. (Overleaf.)

VADVETJÅKKA

Sweden's most northerly national park is one of the most remote in the country and certainly the most inaccessible, especially if you intend to visit the heart of the area. But finding a vantage point from which to see the protected zone is not unduly strenuous. A hiking trail runs for twelve kilometres from the E10 highway almost right to the base of Mount Vádvecohkka, the eleven-hundred-metre-high peak from which the park takes its name. Facing us, the impressive southern slope descends into a lush delta. The trail leads to Vádvevárasi, a small crag on the park border. From here the view is uninterrupted, though we see only the southern part of the protected zone.

The national park comprises a mountain ridge six kilometres long that starts at Mount Vádvecohkka's southern slope and runs all the way to the Norwegian border. To the east of the ridge stands Mount Cuonacohkka, which at one thousand two hundred and forty-seven metres is the lowest mountain in Sweden with a glacier. Two deep valleys flank the ridge on either side and enclose the delta. Hikers who want to continue from here into the national park have to cross one of the two rivers that encircle the park like moats. The rivers form the park boundaries and are formidable natural obstacles with their strong currents and deep gorges. One must hike further upstream, to their calmer tributaries, to find a safe way across.

To the north-west we glimpse the gorge through which one of the two rivers, the Vádvejohka, flows. Steep mountain-faces contrast with the emptier, more expansive scenery to the east. We cannot see the magnificent Lake Torneträsk, but can sense its presence from the light hue of the sky in that direction. The river delta is rich in bird life and home to the sedge warbler, a species uncommon elsewhere in the Swedish uplands.

Light reflects from the lagoons out in the delta and the Njuoraeatnu, the third of Vadvetjåkka's main rivers, meanders between the fens and marshes. Sandbars, clumps of willow bushes and groves of downy birch create a mosaic-like pattern. The lush greenery is almost tropical and the climate not as cold as the Arctic latitude might suggest. The Atlantic

Down the ages the River Vádvejohka has carved a deep ravine in the soft and brittle rock. The famous Gateway of Lapland and Abisko National Park are in the background. Vadvetjåkka National Park starts from the tree-clad slope to the left of the river. Farther upriver, the water flows through a basin-like valley ending in an alpine pass that crosses the Norwegian border. Vadvetjåkka is one of only six Swedish national parks totally undisturbed by exploitation.

Mountain hares occur in the national park. The species gains a white coat in winter.

Dwarf cornel grows in the mountain birch forest. At times the landscape takes on an almost park-like look.

The River Njuoraeatnu feeds a network of lagoons in the Vadvetjåkka delta. Here, a couple of canoes pass through on their way downriver.

Morning mistlingers over the delta beneath Mount Vádvecohkka. The ground here is highly fertile and rich in bird life. A family of reindeer herders lived here from 1850 to 1880, but no sign of their presence remains today. (Overleaf.)

Ocean, with its warming Gulf Stream, is not far away on the other side of the Norwegian border and a major reason why Vadvetjåkka is one of Sweden's wettest places.

Although a national park, Vadvetjåkka is little visited. Indeed, one might well ask why the area was chosen as a national park at all. The answer is history. The conservation pioneers of the early 1900s wanted to set aside the entire area north and north-west of Lake Torneträsk as a national park. But by the time the proposal filtered through to the government only two smaller alternatives remained on the table. Professor Einar Lönnberg, a leading biologist, paid a visit and declared that the area surrounding Mount Vádvecohkka, with its diverse flora and luxuriant delta, was the most interesting area from a conservation standpoint – and recommended its protection as a national park. Parliament officially rubber-stamped his recommendation in 1920.

These days, Vadvetjåkka would be too small to qualify as a national park, but new research has shown that its habitats are more valuable than originally believed. Large limestone caves were discovered in the mountainside in 1978 and are the deepest of their kind in the country. One has an underground waterfall fifty metres high.

REFLECTION

It is just after dawn in May and a pair of red-throated loons swims serenely on Lake Hälletjärn in Tresticklan National Park, the birds' reflections floating dreamlike on the water's surface. Being here in this remote wilderness gives me a feeling of well-being. Concealed behind the lakeside trees I feel at one with these graceful birds, the deep forest, the dark reflections in the water – with the national park. The mood takes me back in time to when ancient forests covered most of Sweden. Tresticklan's miles of unbroken forest have never been fractured by loggers' roads and the trees have stood free from modern-day felling machines. This virgin landscape is why Tresticklan was chosen as a national park and brings to mind Orre-Bryngel, a mysterious trapper who lived here in the nineteenth century. Like me, maybe he also crept stealthily among the trees trying to approach the loons – only he probably had a gun in his hand and was intent on a loon skin for his hat. My mission is entirely peaceful: to take photographs for this book. The idea of pretending to be a trapper appeals to me, not out of nostalgia but because it affords a taste of living in harmony with nature's ebb and flow, as people did in bygone times. Being in nature lets us be present in the moment in a way that busy urban life has taken from us. Nature always has time to pause and catch its breath. Its tempo is slower, more human, and it is here that I am most likely to lose track of time. And it is here, away from the crowds, that one gains perspective on life – a good enough reason, in its own right, for having national parks. These places allow us to experience the tranquil, timeless essence of nature in peace and quiet. National parks are there for us.

There are other reasons. I see myself hiking in Fulufjället National Park and finding a breeding pair of gyrfalcons. As I scan the cliff where they are nesting I hear the whistle of wing beats. This aerial master of the Swedish mountains stoops towards the ledge where four hungry downy chicks gape excitedly. I sit for several hours on a mountainside opposite the nest site, following the comings and goings and waiting long periods for the adults to return with prey in their talons. Most of the time they are

Hallskär, an unusually flat rocky island at Nämdö-skärgården in the outer Stockholm skerries, is a nature reserve and popular spot for day-trippers. Until now, no part of this unique landscape – Sweden's largest outlying archipelago – has enjoyed national park status. But this oversight is about to be remedied and Nämdöskärgården has been proposed as a national park. The designated area is owned by the state and consists of one thousand hectares of land and thirteen thousand hectares of sea.

so fast that they come and go again before I have time to react and press the shutter, but I do eventually get some pictures – a wonderful memory of one of nature's secrets. Why is it so uplifting to watch these falcons rear their young? The selfish view is that it is one's own enjoyment of these beautiful creatures that is the prime motivation. And yet the experience also stirs one's empathy with the birds and their lives. I believe that most nature-lovers recognise these twin feelings. The national park is a haven for vulnerable wildlife and that makes us glad. Strictly speaking, we do not need to see the animals with our own eyes: it is enough to know they are there. The protected zone is there for man and for the gyrfalcon. And the national park, with its animals, plants and geography adds to our appreciation of nature.

I found myself in other similar situations when working on this book, a process that filled me with new experiences and reunited me with past ones. Twenty-five years ago my first book was published and had the same title: *Sweden's National Parks*. I wrote it while working at the Swedish Environmental Protection Agency, and during that time a large part of my job involved national park management and drawing up plans for new parks, especially in the mountains of the far north.

This time I revisited the parks as a photographer. I made numerous trips, some of them to places of which I will never grow tired. The first Swedish national park I ever visited was Stora Sjöfallet. From there, I and a group of teenage friends hiked to Sarek. The alpine peaks, lush birchwoods, mountain vistas and rushing rivers left indelible memories. Back then, we knew little about mountain safety and the risks involved in being out in the wilds, but despite rough weather and too many mosquito bites to count we were hooked for life. I have visited these two national parks almost every year since then, sometimes several times. They are mostly as they were four decades ago, though a few changes are creeping in. Back in the 1970s, the sky above Sarek was always dotted with natural clouds; today they mix with aeroplane contrails. Modern life gets everywhere – even here. On dark nights you can see satellites moving across the Sarek sky, and if you have a global positioning device in your pocket you can check your precise position at any time.

Aeroplane contrails also serve as a metaphor for climate change, the signs of which are readily visible in the mountains. Glaciers are shrinking and the tree-line is encroaching ever further up the mountainsides. What is the point of having national parks if we do not take action against the destruction of our environment? It is a good question, but in my opinion conservation zones are more important than ever if we are to restore the Earth's balance. Our planet needs environments where nature can take its own course as a counterweight to urban sprawl. Establishing national parks can be seen as long-term environmental care while we take the short-term measures necessary to tackle climate change. Both are needed to save the world.

An unnamed glacier on Mount Unna Stuollo in the heart of Sarek National Park, with Rapadalen Valley in the background. Glacial movements have created the moraine ridge to the right. The law of gravity means that glaciers are in perpetual motion: their ice shifts downwards at a rate of thirty to forty metres per year in Sweden. Glacier size is determined by climatic conditions, and the ice in the Swedish mountains has shrunk during the last century. Nowadays we see glaciers and the traces they leave behind them as an archive of climatic change. National parks and the unique protection they give to their environments are crucial not only to conservation interests but also to scientific study.

Stora Sjöfallet, Sarek and Padjelanta national parks overlap and together epitomise Swedish nature at its majestic best. The Gotska Sandön and Haparanda Skärgård national parks have an altogether different allure, with their exotic sandy beaches, while Kosterhavet, Skuleskogen and Stenshuvud offer magnificent elevated sea views. Other national parks preserve that archetypal Swedish landscape – the coniferous forest. Tyresta is a good example. I built tree-houses there in the 1960s, long before it was considered as a national park. Years later, I found myself working for the EPA on the plan that led to Tyresta being established as a national park, and then a few years later was asked to write a book about the place. Fate works in strange ways sometimes.

For all my fondness for those woods of my youth, Muddus remains my personal favourite of the forested parks. With its ancient woodland, deep gorges and sweeping vistas, it is an icon of Swedish nature – and the one I always mention first to people I do not know. And yet, the holy trinity of Sarek-Padjelanta-Stora Sjöfallet is on a different plane altogether. I have been fortunate to visit many famous national parks in different countries around the world, and this trio is up there with the finest. Their untouched beauty, geological and natural variation, sheer size and magnificent scenery ensure them a place in the premier league of world national parks – as recognised by UNESCO when it declared the area a world heritage site.

Sweden's national park network remains a work in progress. But although new areas have been proposed to make it more comprehensive, I still feel the parks offer a surprisingly representative cross-section of Swedish wildlife and countryside. Among them we find outstanding examples of the country's quintessential physical geography and main habitats: forests, bogs and mountain landscapes. Only the unique coastal archipelagos are under-represented, though hopefully this will be resolved in the future. The recent establishment of Kosterhavet National Park provides a valuable addition to our marine heritage.

When working on this book and travelling from park to park it was deeply inspiring to witness the way the landscapes shift and change. Scenery is the primary visual motif but also the hardest for a photographer to capture. Although the coniferous forests of Tiveden, Tyresta or Tresticklan may look much the same, they differ subtly in their topography and vegetation. My aim was to portray the special spirit of each place while also depicting the mood created by changes in the time of day, weather or season. Photography can be said to fall into two categories: personally expressive images on the one hand, and descriptive and more objective renderings on the other. I often straddle these two approaches. For me, the most powerful themes are those that best epitomise an area and communicate the essence of its nature as I perceive it. The interface between the typical and the unique in a national park is another fascinating aspect. As human beings we are always attracted by variations from what is normal or expected.

A rare bird or flower invariably arouses greater interest than the presence of commoner species – an instinctive and understandable reaction but one that can be misleading when describing a place. I have tried to do justice to each national park in terms of this balance between the typical and the untypical. I also thought it was important that the photographs were taken on location: a few exceptions were necessary for some of the species, but the vast majority of pictures were taken especially for this book.

According to a recent opinion poll, most Swedes know the name of at least one of their national parks – Sarek. The fact that this doyen of Swedish national parks is also the best known is revealing in this era of non-stop information and competition for the spotlight. Extremes tend to attract the most attention. Sarek's place in the public eye strengthens my faith in the importance of national parks. From a conservation standpoint, it is crucial that we retain areas with extra-strong protection and stature. Yet it is not the legal status of national parks that counts most, but rather their communicative power. Most businesses see a value in having flagships that can add a little glamour and colour and are recognisable to the general public. This is the vital role that national parks fill on behalf of conservation.

St Bernard's lily growing in Stenshuvud National Park. This declining flower survives at a couple of dozen sites in Skåne and roughly as many on the island of Öland, as well as at a few other sites in the southern third of Sweden. It grows in sandy steppe-like habitats like the heath at Stenshuvud but is vulnerable to encroaching vegetation and relies on livestock grazing to keep the landscape open. This is an example of how national parks can serve as a haven for endangered species that require active land management.

THE PARKS IN BRIEF

STENSHUVUD
Location: Near Kivik, Skåne county
Established: 1986
Area: 380 hectares
Special features: High coastal hill and long sandy beach
Main habitats: Beechwoods, open heath, sandy coastline
Interesting animals: Sand lizard, tree frog, icterine warbler, common rosefinch, golden oriole, many butterfly species
Interesting plants: Spring flowers, wood anemone, yellow anemone, sweet woodruff, ramson, coralroot bittercress, St Bernard's lily, early marsh-orchid, pasque flower
Activities: Walks, swimming, picnics
Sights: View from Stenshuvud and Kortelshuvud, Sandane heath, beach
Tourism facilities: Nature centre with exhibition and cafeteria, walking trails
Getting there: By road to the northern, central and southern entrances

DALBY SÖDERSKOG
Location: Ten kilometres east of Lund, Skåne county
Established: 1918
Area: 37 hectares
Special features: Dense deciduous woodland
Main habitats: Broadleaf forest
Interesting animals: Stock dove, blackcap, tawny owl, thrush nightingale
Interesting plants: Spring flowers, white anemone, yellow anemone, bird-in-a-bush, dog's mercury
Activities: Walks
Sights: Forest
Tourism facilities: Walking trails
Getting there: By road to a car park at the entrance

SÖDERÅSEN
Location: South of Ljungbyhed, Skåne county
Established: 2001
Area: 1,625 hectares
Special features: Deep gullies and extensive beechwoods
Main habitats: Gullies, beech forest
Interesting animals: Polecat, fallow deer, grey wagtail, hawfinch, lesser spotted woodpecker, European brook lamprey, beetles
Interesting plants: Yellow anemone, enchanter's nightshade, ramson, sanicle, horse's hoof fungus, fungi, lichens and mosses
Activities: Walks, hiking
Sights: View from Kopparhatten, Skäralid Gorge, Nackarpsdalen Valley and Lake Odensjön
Tourism facilities: Nature centre and cafeteria at Skäralid, many trails
Getting there: Trunk road 13 to Skäralid

STORE MOSSE
Location: North-west of Värnamo, Jönköping county
Established: 1982
Area: 7,850 hectares
Special features: Extensive bogs
Main habitats: Bogs, coniferous and deciduous forest, enclosed pasture
Interesting animals: Ducks and wading birds, slavonian grebe, whooper swan, common crane, short-eared owl
Interesting plants: Orchids such as narrow-leaved marsh orchid, fragrant orchid, marsh helleborine
Activities: Walking, hiking, skiing
Sights: View from Björnakullen, Svartgölen Mere, Lake Kävsjön, rural landscape at Svänö and Lövö, sand dunes at Rockne
Tourism facilities: Birdwatching platforms south and north of Lake Kävsjön, hostels at Svänö and Lövö, paths accessible for the disabled, hiking trails
Getting there: County road 151 passes through the park. Small one-way roads to Lövö and Svänö

NORRA KVILL
Location: North of Vimmerby, Kalmar county
Established: 1927, enlarged in 1984
Area: 111 hectares
Special features: Magnificent ancient forest
Main habitats: Ancient coniferous forest, small lakes
Interesting animals: Bats, pine marten, hazelhen
Interesting plants: Hepatica, spring pea, early dog-violet, bush vetch, bog arum, tufted loosestrife
Activities: Walks
Sights: View from Idhöjden, Stora Idgölen
Tourism facilities: Walking trails
Getting there: Minor roads north from Vimmerby

BLÅ JUNGFRUN
Location: In the middle of northern Kalmar Sound
Established: 1926
Area: 198 hectares
Special features: Unusual tall island of red granite
Main habitats: Flat rocks, sparse pine forest, deciduous woods
Interesting animals: Black guillemot, cormorant, northern eider, grass snake
Interesting plants: Woodruff, black pea, angular Solomon's-seal
Activities: Walks, swimming
Sights: View from highest point of the island, Lervikshamn and Sikhamn harbours
Tourism facilities: Day visitors only
Getting there: Ferryboat from Oskarshamn or Byxelkrok

KOSTERHAVET
Location: West of Strömstad, Västra Götaland county
Established: 2009
Area: 38,900 hectares, approx. 300 islands and skerries, ocean
Special features: Barren outlying archipelago and biologically diverse marine environment
Main habitats: Undersea environment, bare islets, flat rocks, grazed coastal meadows

Interesting animals: Harbour seal, northern eider, arctic skua, marine life, migratory birds
Interesting plants: Sea holly, large-leaved linden, alkali buttercup, marine plants
Activities: Sailing, swimming
Sights: Ursholmarna islands, northern Nordkoster, southern Sydkoster
Tourism facilities: Nature centre on Sydkoster
Getting there: Ferryboat from Strömstad

TRESTICKLAN

Location: North of Ed, Västra Götaland county
Established: 1996
Area: 2,909 hectares
Special features: Extensive wild coniferous forest
Main habitats: Coniferous forest, lakes, bogs
Interesting animals: Wolf, European nightjar, red-throated loon
Interesting plants: Bell-heather
Activities: Walks, hiking, skiing, canoeing
Sights: View from Orshöjden, Lake Stora Tresticklan and Lake Lilla Tresticklan
Tourism facilities: A few trails
Getting there: Turning from road between Ed and Nössemark

DJURÖ

Location: Middle of Lake Vänern, Västra Götaland county
Established: 1991
Area: 2,400 hectares, of which 315 are land
Special features: Isolated group of islands in Sweden's largest lake
Main habitats: Freshwater, forested islands, barren islets
Interesting animals: Fallow deer, white-tailed eagle, osprey, hobby, common tern, greylag goose
Interesting plants: Shore plants
Activities: Boating, sailing, canoeing and walks
Sights: Hunting lodge at Djurö, island of Gisslan
Tourism facilities: A few trails, marina
Getting there: Private boat

TIVEDEN

Location: Between Lake Vättern and Lake Vänern, Västra Götaland and Örebro counties
Established: 1983
Area: 1,353 hectares, due to be enlarged
Special features: Rocky and hilly old coniferous forest
Main habitats: Coniferous forest, forest lakes, bogs
Interesting animals: Pine marten, capercaillie, hazelhen, three-toed woodpecker, beetles
Interesting plants: Sparse flora
Activities: Swimming, walks, hiking, skiing
Sights: Stenkälla sacrificial site, view from Stora Trollkyrka, Stigmanspasset (Highwayman Pass), rock of Junker the Hunter, Vitsand beach
Tourism facilities: Many hiking trails
Getting there: Minor road from trunk road 49

GOTSKA SANDÖN

Location: North of Fårö, Gotland county
Established: 1909, enlarged in 1963 and again with a 300-metre coastal zone in 1988
Area: 4,500 hectares, of which 3,658 are land
Special features: Isolated sandy island with untouched beaches and unique pinewoods
Main habitats: Sandy beaches, pine forest, small deciduous groves
Interesting animals: Grey seal, blue hare, golden eagle, beetles
Interesting plants: Red helleborine, sword-leaved helleborine, marsh helleborine, sea rocket
Activities: Swimming, walks
Sights: Bredsand, Höga Land, Franska Bukten, Las Palmas, Höga Åsen, Gamla Gården
Tourism facilities: Accommodation (tents, cabins or houses) must be booked in advance. Roads for walking
Getting there: Ferries from Nynäshamn and Fårö

TYRESTA

Location: Twenty kilometres south of Stockholm, Stockholm county
Established: 1993
Area: 1,970 hectares
Special features: Rare ancient coniferous forest with large fire-ravaged areas
Main habitats: Primeval coniferous forest, fire-ravaged areas, rocky ground, forest lakes, small mires
Interesting animals: Eagle owl, pygmy owl, European nightjar, lesser spotted woodpecker, red-throated loon
Interesting plants: Umbellate wintergreen, bog orchid, mosses, lichens, fungi
Activities: Walks, hiking, skiing
Sights: Tyresta village, fire areas, primeval forest
Tourism facilities: National park buildings, many well marked trails
Getting there: By road from Haninge, bus service

ÄNGSÖ

Location: South of Norrtälje, Stockholm county
Established: 1909
Area: 188 hectares, of which 77 are land
Special features: Traditional rural landscape
Main habitats: Meadows and pastures, coniferous forest, reedbeds
Interesting animals: White-tailed eagle, osprey, great crested grebe
Interesting plants: Elder-flowered orchid, early marsh-orchid, butterfly orchis, ramson, sweet woodruff
Activities: Boating, sailing, swimming, walks, picnics
Sights: Stormaren meadow, Hemudden, Svartviken
Tourism facilities: Tourist jetty with nature centre, trails
Getting there: Private boat

GARPHYTTAN

Location: Twenty kilometres west of Örebro, Örebro county
Established: 1909
Area: 111 hectares
Special features: Traditional rural landscape
Main habitats: Meadows
Interesting animals: Dormouse, northern birch mouse, smooth snake
Interesting plants: Spring flowers, columbine, buttercup
Activities: Walks, picnics
Sights: Stenlyckan, view from Svensbodaberget
Tourism facilities: Walking and hiking trails
Getting there: Turn-off from E18 highway

FÄRNEBOFJÄRDEN

Location: River Dalälven, 40 kilometres south of Sandviken at the juncture of Dalarna, Västmanland and Gävleborg counties

Established: 1998
Area: 10,100 hectares, of which 5,990 are land
Special features: Varied riverside with extensive forests
Main habitats: Riverside beaches, rapids, rivers, coniferous forest, bogs
Interesting animals: Lynx, Ural owl, osprey, hobby, hazelhen, capercaillie, white-backed woodpecker, grey-headed woodpecker, beetles
Interesting plants: Fen violet, black pea, Solomon's-seal, lichens and fungi
Activities: Hiking, boating, sailing, canoeing, long-distance skating, skiing, fishing
Sights: Rapids at Tyttbo and Gysinge, viewing platform at Skekarsbo, River Storån, islands of Sandön and Tisjön
Tourism facilities: Viewing platform
Getting there: Trunk road 56 passes Gysinge; other access via minor roads

HAMRA

Location: Eight kilometres north-east of Tandsjöborg, Gävleborg county
Established: 1909, enlarged in 2011
Area: 1383 hectares
Special features: Small genuine ancient forest
Main habitats: Coniferous forest, mire
Interesting animals: Brown bear, otter, woodpeckers, beetles
Interesting plants: White beak-sedge, creeping lady's tresses, lesser twayblade
Activities: Walks
Sights: Näckrostjärnen Lake
Tourism facilities: Trail
Getting there: Minor road five kilometres from trunk road 81

FULUFJÄLLET

Location: Twenty kilometres west of Särna, Dalarna county
Established: 2002
Area: 38,485 hectares
Special features: Mountain fells with unique geology and ungrazed bushy ground
Main habitats: Alpine plateau, coniferous forest, upland birch forest, mire
Interesting animals: Brown bear, beaver, gyrfalcon, golden eagle, whimbrel, moths, snails
Interesting plants: Mosses and lichens
Activities: Walks, hiking, skiing, fishing
Sights: Njupeskär waterfall, River Göljån's lower reaches, altar rails at Storhön
Tourism facilities: Nature centre and well marked trail to Njupeskär, hiking trails
Getting there: Minor road from trunk road 70

TÖFSINGDALEN

Location: Thirty-five kilometres north of Idre, Dalarna county
Established: 1930
Area: 1,615 hectares
Special features: Forest strewn with giant boulders
Main habitats: Coniferous forest with boulders, patches of birch forest and upland moor
Interesting animals: Brown bear, dipper, beaver, wood warbler, garden warbler, three-toed woodpecker
Interesting plants: Baneberry, large white buttercup, wolf lichen
Activities: Hiking, skiing
Sights: View from Hovden and deadwood there, River Storån
Tourism facilities: Short trail
Getting there: Remote and inaccessible

SONFJÄLLET

Location: Fifteen kilometres south of Hede, Jämtland county
Established: 1909, enlarged in 1988
Area: 10,440 hectares
Special features: Graceful alpine massif with unique geology and a few grazed moors
Main habitats: Alpine mountains, upland birch forest, coniferous forest, bogs
Interesting animals: Brown bear, lynx, pine marten, birds of prey
Interesting plants: Lichens
Activities: Hiking, skiing
Sights: View from Högfjället and Korpflyet, Sododalen
Tourism facilities: Nature centre at Nyvallen, hiking trails
Getting there: Roads to Nyvallen in the east and Nysätern in the west

SKULESKOGEN

Location: Forty kilometres south of Örnsköldsvik, Västernorrland county
Established: 1984, enlarged in 2009
Area: 3062 hectares
Special features: Majestic high coast with ancient coniferous forest
Main habitats: Coniferous forest, flat rocks
Interesting animals: Lynx, grey-headed woodpecker, willow grouse
Interesting plants: Southern species like linden and hazel, mezereon, Methuselah's beard lichen
Activities: Walks, hiking, swimming
Sights: Slåttdalsskrevan ravine, view from Slåttdalsberget, Tärnättholmarna

Tourism facilities: Hiking trails, sleeping cabins
Getting there: Minor roads to the northern and southern entrances

BJÖRNLANDET

Location: Twenty kilometres south of Fredrika, Västerbotten county
Established: 1991, due to be expanded
Area: 1,130 hectares
Special features: Unspoilt taiga, rolling terrain
Main habitats: Coniferous forest, bogs
Interesting animals: Woodpeckers, brown bear, owls
Interesting plants: Alpine blue-sow-thistle, toothed wintergreen
Activities: Walks
Sights: View from Mount Björnberget
Tourism facilities: A few trails
Getting there: Minor roads from trunk road 92

HAPARANDA SKÄRGÅRD

Location: South of Haparanda, Norrbotten county
Established: 1995
Area: 6,000 hectares, of which 770 are land
Special features: Scattered sandy islands with unusual vegetation
Main habitats: Sandy beaches, heaths, pinewoods
Interesting animals: Grey seal, ringed seal, migratory birds, arctic tern, red-breasted merganser
Interesting plants: Sea buckthorn, sea pea, sea rocket, field dock
Activities: Boating, sailing, walks, swimming
Sights: Sandskär and the Kumpula fishing hamlet

Tourism facilities: Trails
Getting there: Private boat

PIELJEKAISE
Location: Six kilometres south of Jäkkvik, Norrbotten county
Established: 1909, enlarged 1913
Area: 15,340 hectares
Special features: Expansive untouched upland birch forest
Main habitats: Upland birch forest, bogs, barren fells
Interesting animals: Common scoter, golden eagle, great snipe
Interesting plants: Birch forest meadows with alpine blue-sow-thistle, northern wolfsbane and globe-flower
Activities: Hiking, skiing
Sights: View from Pieljekaise and Baktek
Tourism facilities: The Royal Trail, hostel
Getting there: Trunk road 95 to Jäkkvik, bus service

MUDDUS
Location: Approx. 40 kilometres south-west of Gällivare, Norrbotten county
Established: 1942, enlarged 1984
Area: 49,340 hectares
Special features: Taiga with large bogs and deep gorges
Main habitats: Coniferous forest, bogs
Interesting animals: Pine marten, lynx, brown bear, bean goose, whooper swan, smew, pintail, hen harrier
Interesting plants: Fairy slipper, ghost orchid, marsh saxifrage, alpine lady-fern, arctic lychnis, manycleft potentilla
Activities: Hiking, skiing
Sights: Muddusluobbal, Muddusfallet waterfall, River Måskoskårså
Tourism facilities: Hiking trail

with sleeping cabins
Getting there: Minor road from E45 highway at Ligga

STORA SJÖFALLET
Location: Ninety kilometres north-west of Porjus, Norrbotten county
Established: 1909, reduced in size in 1919
Area: 127,800 hectares
Special features: Majestic alpine landscape with high peaks and montane plateaus
Main habitats: Alpine fells, upland birch forest, boulders and glaciers
Interesting animals: White-tailed eagle, gyrfalcon, long-tailed duck, purple sandpiper
Interesting plants: Lapland rosebay, rooted poppy
Activities: Hiking, skiing
Sights: Áhkkà and Kallak-tjåkkå massifs, Teusadalen
Tourism facilities: The Royal Trail crosses the northern part of the park
Getting there: Ritsemvägen Road, a turnoff from the E45 highway, passes through the park

SAREK
Location: Ten kilometres north of Kvikkjokk, Norrbotten county
Established: 1909, enlarged 1962
Area: 197,000 hectares
Special features: Magnificent and high alpine area with steep peaks, deep valleys and a rich delta
Main habitats: Alpine environments, boulder fields, glaciers, upland birch forest, fells with low bushy undergrowth, pine forest
Interesting animals: Brown bear, wolverine, lynx, gyrfalcon, golden eagle, whooper swan
Interesting plants: Rock

speedwell, mountain avens, arctic bellflower, rooted poppy
Activities: Hiking, skiing
Sights: Rapaselet, Skierffe, Bierikjávvrre, Sarvesvágge, Luohttoláhko, Njoatsosvággi
Tourism facilities: Several bridges
Getting there: Twenty or so kilometres by foot from Kvikkjokk to the south or Änonjalme to the north

PADJELANTA
Location: West of Sarek National Park, Norrbotten county
Established: 1962
Area: 198,400 hectares
Special features: Extensive rolling fells, large lakes
Main habitats: Fell
Interesting animals: Arctic fox, golden eagle, velvet scoter, long-tailed duck, merlin, gyrfalcon
Interesting plants: Dwarf mountain cinquefoil, redrattle, rock speedwell
Activities: Hiking, skiing
Sights: Sårjåsjaure cabin, Staloluokta, Jiegnáffo, Jávrregasska
Tourism facilities: Padjelanta Trail and sleeping cabins
Getting there: By air to Staloluokta, 20 or so kilometres by foot from Änonjalme

ABISKO
Location: South of Torneträsk, Norrbotten county
Established: 1909
Area: 7,700 hectares
Special features: Wide mountain valley with upland birch forest and river gorge
Main habitats: Upland birch forest
Interesting animals: Garden warbler, arctic warbler, whimbrel, greenshank

Interesting plants: Blunt-leaved orchid, Lapland rosebay, yellow alpine milkvetch, arctic bell-heather
Activities: Walks, hiking, skiing
Sights: Abiskojåkka Gorge, midnight sun on Mount Njulla, Rihtonjira, Ábeskojávri
Tourism facilities: Royal Trail, Abisko Mountain Station, ski lift on Mount Njulla
Getting there: E10 highway and railway pass the northern perimeter of the park

VADVETJÅKKA
Location: North-west of Torneträsk, Norrbottens county
Established: 1920
Area: 2,630 hectares
Special features: Mountain ridge with large caves and a large delta area
Main habitats: Upland birch forest, upland fell
Interesting animals: Sedge warbler, arctic redpoll, ring ouzel, Eurasian wigeon, greater scaup
Interesting plants: Northern primrose, rock speedwell, yellow saxifrage, purple saxifrage
Activities: Hiking, skiing
Sights: Delta area, Cunujohka and Vádvejohka gorges
Tourism facilities: None
Getting there: Ten-kilometre hike from the E10 highway

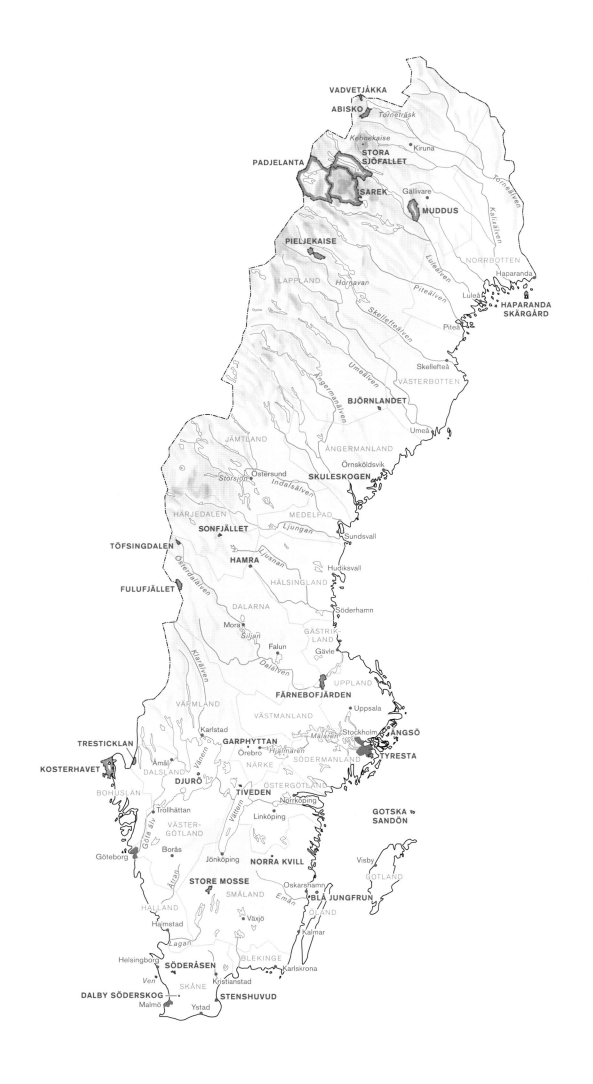

VADVETJÅKKA

ABISKO
Torneträsk

Kebnekaise
• Kiruna

**STORA
SJÖFALLET**

PADJELANTA

SAREK
Gällivare

MUDDUS

PIELJEKAISE

LAPPLAND
Hornavan

NORRBOTTEN

Luleälven

Piteälven

Skellefteälven

Haparanda

Luleå

Piteå

**HAPARANDA
SKÄRGÅRD**

Umeälven

VÄSTERBOTTEN

Skellefteå

Ångermanälven

BJÖRNLANDET

Umeå

JÄMTLAND

ÅNGERMANLAND

Örnsköldsvik

Östersund

SKULESKOGEN

Storsjön

Indalsälven

HÄRJEDALEN

MEDELPAD

SONFJÄLLET

Ljungan

Sundsvall

TÖFSINGDALEN

Ljusnan

Hudiksvall

HAMRA

HÄLSINGLAND

FULUFJÄLLET

Österdalälven

DALARNA

Söderhamn

GÄSTRIK-
LAND

Mora

Siljan

Falun

Gävle

Dalälven

Klarälven

UPPLAND

FÄRNEBOFJÄRDEN

VÄRMLAND

Uppsala

VÄSTMANLAND

Karlstad

GARPHYTTAN

Mälaren

Stockholm

ÄNGSÖ

TRESTICKLAN

Örebro

Hjälmaren

TYRESTA

Åmål

Vänern

SÖDERMANLAND

KOSTERHAVET

DALSLAND

NÄRKE

DJURÖ

ÖSTERGÖTLAND

TIVEDEN

BOHUSLÄN

Norrköping

Trollhättan

Vättern

Linköping

**GOTSKA
SANDÖN**

VÄSTER-
GÖTLAND

Göta älv

Borås

NORRA KVILL

Göteborg

Jönköping

Visby

STORE MOSSE

GOTLAND

Ätran

SMÅLAND

Oskarshamn

Emån

BLÅ JUNGFRUN

HALLAND

Växjö

ÖLAND

Halmstad

Kalmar

Lagan

Helsingborg

BLEKINGE

SÖDERÅSEN

Karlskrona

Ven

SKÅNE

Kristianstad

DALBY SÖDERSKOG

STENSHUVUD

Malmö

Ystad